HOW TO ...

garden and grow: gardening as therapy for children with SEND

Becky Pinniger

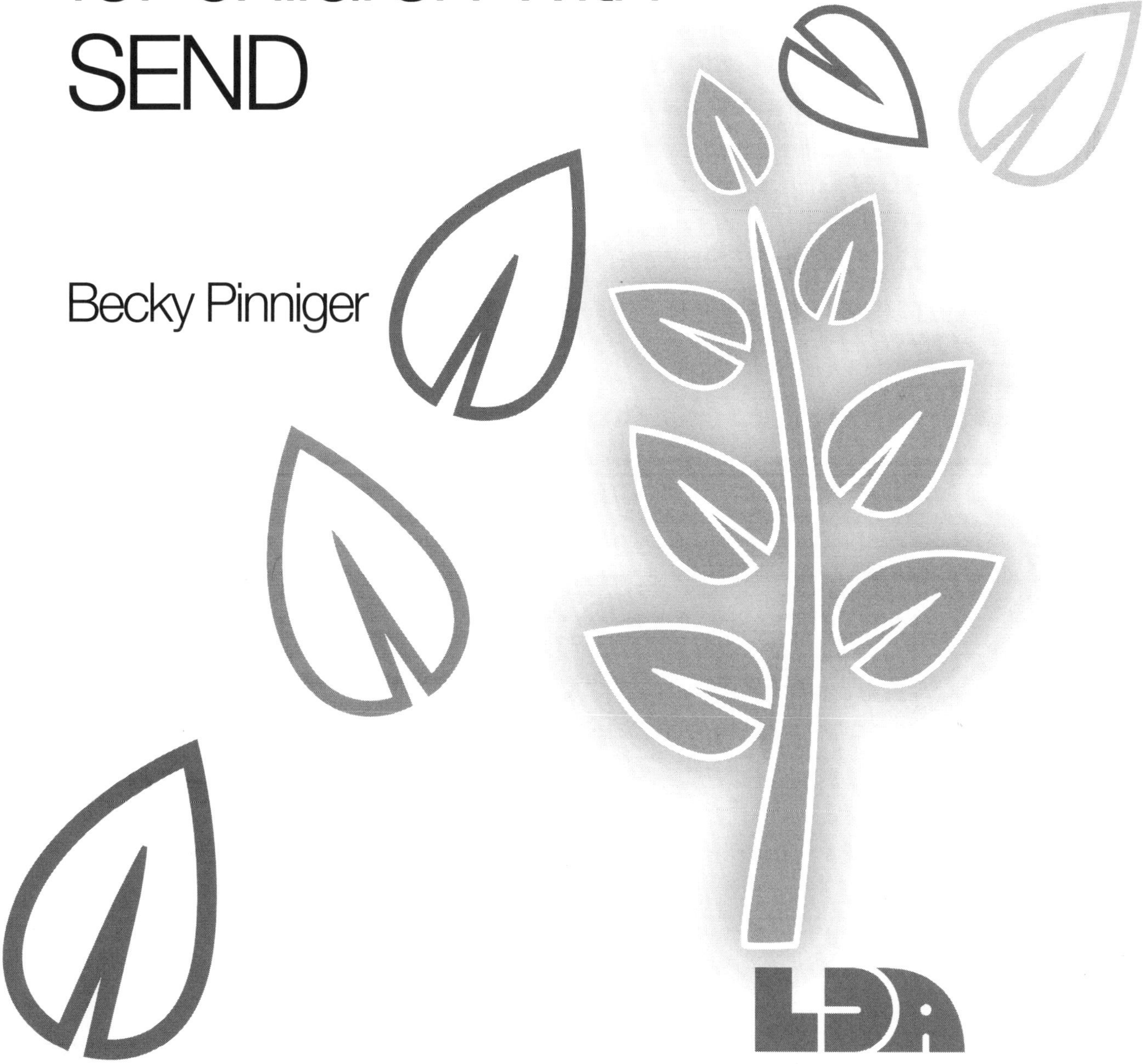

LDA

How to garden and grow: gardening as therapy for children with SEND
ISBN: 978-1-85503-596-6

© Becky Pinniger 2015
Illustrations by Becky Pinniger

This edition published 2015
10 9 8 7 6 5

Printed in the UK by Page Bros (Norwich) Ltd
Designed and typeset by Andy Wilson for Green Desert Ltd

LDA, 2 Gregory Street, Hyde, Cheshire SK14 4HR

www.ldalearning.com

The right of Becky Pinniger to be identified as the author of this work has been asserted in accordance with Sections 77 and 78 of the Copyright, Designs and Patents Act 1988.

All rights reserved. This book contains materials which may be reproduced by photocopier or other means for use by the purchaser. The permission is granted on the understanding that these copies will be used within the educational establishment of the purchaser. The book and all its contents remain copyright. Copies may be made without reference to the publisher or the licensing scheme for the making of photocopies operated by the Publishers Licensing Society.

CONTENTS

	Acknowledgements	iv
	Introduction Why garden?	1
1	Child-centred gardening	9
2	Gardening: the basics	20
3	What to keep in your 'shed'	42
4	Garden design considerations	48
5	Sensory integration in the garden	55
6	Garden-related activities and games	64
7	Assessing the value of gardening	80
8	A year-round programme of activities and tasks in the garden	86
9	A seasonal programme with learning outcomes	103
10	Developing a scheme of work	108
	Glossary	113
	Sources of information	118
	References	122

CD-ROM contains

Appendix A A list of plants and their qualities

Appendix B Picture prompts and ideas for games

ACKNOWLEDGEMENTS

The inspiration and energy for this book have come from the wonderful children and young people I have been fortunate enough to work with and introduce to the joys of gardening. The therapists and other staff at Thrive have been a source of encouragement and ideas. Working at the Thrive garden in Reading has been a life-changing experience. The impetus for the book has come from running workshops for Thrive, where there was evident need for a book to cover the many aspects of gardening with children with SEND. Friend and colleague Chris Jones at Addington Special School badgered me in the kindest possible way to keep on with the book when I struggled.

I am grateful to the editorial team at LDA, Megan Crowe and Juliet West, for their interest in the book, and for the kindness and patience of Yvonne Percival when doing the copy-editing.

Special thanks are due to David, Edward and Lucy for their constant support and diligent proofreading, without which this book may well have been composted.

INTRODUCTION
Why garden?

We believe that every young person should experience the world beyond the classroom as an essential part of learning and personal development, whatever their age, ability or circumstances.
(DfES, 2006)

There are many books available on gardening with children, which are well illustrated, full of clear instructions and ideas for seasonal activities. These books are aimed at children, parents and teachers and can be a mine of information.

There are, however, very few gardening books written particularly for those working with children recognised as having special educational needs and/or disability (SEND). Their specific need or disability may restrict their opportunities to venture into a garden and be involved in any activities. Consequently, some are being *excluded* from the many and varied benefits that being outdoors and involved in gardening can bring.

As a horticultural therapist working with children of different needs and ages, I am aware of just how therapeutic and beneficial gardening can be for them. I have worked with teachers, teaching assistants, parents and volunteers, to enable them to garden with their children with SEND, and it has made me aware of the need for a practical guide book. That is why I have written this book. I hope it will make it easier for carers to enable all children, whatever their ability, to benefit in some way through the wonderful resources of gardens, gardening and the natural environment.

Horticultural therapy

The idea of using gardening, or horticulture, as a therapy to improve wellbeing, mood and the general welfare of people is a well-established one. Taken in its simplest form, merely being outside, enjoying the greenery and surroundings can be therapeutic, and may involve active or passive participation. When gardening is used to address a particular need of an individual, it is recognised as **horticultural therapy**.

A garden environment is the ideal place to aid the **attention restoration*** that some children need. Here they can restore their equilibrium, clear their mind and settle their anxieties. This can be achieved by the 'soft fascination' of looking at their surroundings, sitting by a pond, going for a walk over the soft grass, or smelling leaves and flowers (Kaplan and Kaplan, 1989).

* Terms in **bold** can be found in the Glossary.

Wilson (1984) first identified this human need to 'affiliate with life and lifelike processes', which he termed the 'biophilia effect'. Children and adults alike benefit from contact with nature, which has been reduced because of lifestyles today. Getting children involved in gardens and gardening is one way to reap the restorative benefit of these natural environments.

Whether children have SEND or not, there are enormous benefits for them just from being outdoors, whether in a garden, park or woods. Giving them a place in which to garden can be even more beneficial.

According to the Code of Practice: 'A pupil has SEN where their learning difficulty or disability calls for special educational provision, namely provision different from or additional to that normally available to pupils of the same age' (DfE, 2015, p. 94). Children with SEND are generally included in one or more of the following categories:

- general learning
- sensory impairment
- physical disabilities, including those with profound and multiple learning disabilities (PMLD)
- speech and language impairment
- developmental delay
- emotional and behavioural difficulties
- social and communication difficulties
- severe allergies
- autistic spectrum – which may include many of the above.

The needs of disengaged young people are addressed in this book too, although they may not come under the SEND umbrella.

Inevitably it is easier for some, more than others, to access outdoor spaces, gardens and gardening itself. This book aims to address how children with SEND can benefit from gardens and gardening, and how you can make it possible for *all* children to do so.

By working in gardens with young people, therapists at Thrive (a registered charity using social and **therapeutic horticulture** to benefit those touched by disability) have demonstrated how children with SEND can benefit. Anecdotal evidence gathered from parents, staff and the young people themselves has shown what a positive experience coming to the garden and being involved in gardening can be. Their confidence, independence and awareness of the world around them can be improved by gardening for a few hours a week. Some young people have the additional benefit of being given a purpose and direction in which to go after leaving school.

Socialising

The Royal Horticultural Society (RHS) also uses horticulture with children with special needs. Its project 'Moving Up, Growing On' demonstrated clearly how horticulture can change the lives and prospects of many young people with SEND, including those who become disaffected with school.

Benefits of gardens and gardening

As explained below, the benefits of gardening can include:

- improvement in physical health
- improvement in psychological health
- social benefits
- access to the environment and connecting with nature
- qualifications and skills development.

Reduce anxiety and enable 'attention restoration'

Providing an open outdoor space enables anxious children, or those whose concentration has tired, to feel rested, safe and calm.

Children on the autistic spectrum are among those who often experience high levels of anxiety. This can be so overwhelming that the children are unable to receive information or take part in activities. Trying to engage a child in this state is almost impossible and bound to end in frustration all round. For such a child, 'attention restoration' (Kaplan and Kaplan, 1989) is the key.

Use the outside space to find a way to reduce the anxiety. Perhaps provide a sheltered space to sit, where, if they are left undisturbed, children can listen to the gentle sound of water, or lie on the grass under a tree and observe the leaves blowing and watch the clouds moving across the sky. These natural features can be observed effortlessly, their mind can rest, they can relax and their ability to concentrate can be 'restored'. Going for a walk, or observing wildlife coming to the feeders or purpose-built bug houses, can also be effective in achieving this.

Attention restoration

Those children who are generally hyperactive and with poor focus have been shown to improve concentration for longer periods if they are outdoors. Children stressed by their efforts to focus in the classroom can likewise be calmed if they spend time outside in this process of 'attention restoration'.

Reduce anger and frustration and improve overall fitness

Being outdoors in the fresh air and expending energy can enable children to dispel anger and frustrations. For example, children with attention deficit (hyperactivity) disorder (ADHD) or emotional difficulties may improve their focus and mood and reduce adrenalin levels by engaging in vigorous physical tasks, such as digging over a vegetable bed. Other physical tasks, such as filling and pushing a laden wheelbarrow, raking bark, carrying and stacking bricks, and turning or spreading **compost**, are equally helpful.

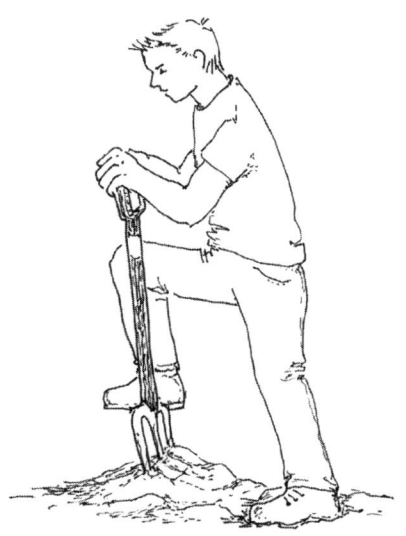

Physical effort can be beneficial for both physical and mental wellbeing

Make an obstacle course around which to wheel the barrows, or have wheelbarrow manoeuvring competitions. Such activities will also help to keep the children physically fit. In an age when children can spend between seven and eight hours a day in sedentary activities or in front of a screen, encouraging meaningful tasks using physical effort is beneficial for both their physical and mental wellbeing.

Provide a place to play and use imagination

Play can be defined as activities freely chosen by the child – that is, they are voluntary activities, following the child's own ideas and interests, in their own way, for their own reasons.

The benefits of play cannot be overestimated. In 1999, the Mental Health Foundation reported that the limited opportunities that children have to play outside were the cause of increased mental ill health among young people. Some children are missing out on play for a variety of reasons, including the limiting factors of their condition. Play is the child's way of making sense of the world and, above all, should be *fun*. There are no goals to be achieved; it is the *process* that is important (see National Children's Bureau, 1992 and Sources of information).

There is plenty of evidence, both past and present, to support the notion that play is vital for the cognitive, emotional, social and physical development of children. Play enables children to develop **gross motor skills** and **fine motor skills**, social skills and language; it is a vital ingredient for all learning. It can be particularly important for those children who have missed out on play experiences in their early years because of global developmental delay, sensory impairment or severe learning difficulties.

A garden is the perfect place to provide opportunities for play, and ideally a garden will be designed with this in mind. Play provides the foundation stones on which all other learning can be based. Without it there may be gaps in understanding. Children with emotional problems, or disengaged young people who are struggling academically, may also enjoy nothing more than messy play. It enables them to relax and be a child once more, and if it can be incorporated as a real task, then they are not embarrassed by it. For example, provide a bowl of warm soapy water, plenty of dirty pots, old washing-up brushes, add in a couple of 'disaffected youngsters' and stand well back. They will have a great time, splashing each other and creating bubbles – and, with any luck, they will clean the pots at the same time.

Enable children to use their imagination and build camps, or create artworks from twigs, leaves, cones, and so on. Instead of construction toys, puzzles and paint, provide pieces of log, assorted flowerpots, labels, stones, sand, compost, water, funnels, buckets, berries to squash (excellent natural paint, applied with sticks) – anything to sort and build, pour and wash and otherwise play with. Provide a safe space for play and ensure that adults are involved as little as possible. Ideally, part of the garden should be left as a wilderness, in which the children can explore and investigate the natural world and use their imagination.

Flowerpots can make good construction toys

Encourage communication and socialisation

It is possible to provide opportunities for meaningful conversation and communication through various activities, as well as play. The previous examples of play provide natural opportunities to encourage these. Structured sessions, such as sharing a plot together, planning what to grow, and sharing tasks with multiple steps can all encourage communication and socialisation. The children and task must always be chosen carefully, because 'teamwork' can be fraught both for participants and the adult leader, depending on the needs of the children.

Structured sessions provide opportunities for communication and socialisation

A good way to start communication and socialisation is working one-to-one with an 'unsocial' child. Being side by side at the work bench, or on a plot, or just having a walk around the garden together provides a non-threatening environment in which to have a two-way conversation. The parent of an autistic young man said that the only place she ever had what amounted to a conversation with her son, was when they sat around the pond in the garden, watching goldfish.

Getting a group together at the beginning and end of working sessions gives a natural opportunity for conversation about what they have been doing, what they would like to do, or what they enjoy doing. At the end of the day, children can describe what they have enjoyed or found difficult. As a child's confidence increases, they may feel able to initiate the group meeting sessions, and this can further boost their self-esteem. Ensure that listening to others is as much part of the process as asking questions of each other. For those children unable to communicate verbally, their preferred method of communication, for example **Makaton**, **PECS** (the Picture Exchange Communication System) or **Widget symbols**, could be used. A simple picture communication system has been used at Thrive for many children who may not be used to PECS, enabling them to choose their preferred activity. See Appendix B on the CD-ROM.

Improve strength and co-ordination

Provide opportunities for strengthening limbs and for developing, through tasks, children's co-ordination, and the use of both sides of the body. Some children on the autistic spectrum may have **hypersensitivities** or **hyposensitivities** in their **vestibular** and **proprioceptive systems**, related to their sense of balance. These systems also affect their awareness of their body in space and their co-ordination. The garden can provide opportunities for those with reduced sensitivities to rock or spin, using a rope or swing attached to a tree for example. Children who are oversensitive in this way may need places in which to be still.

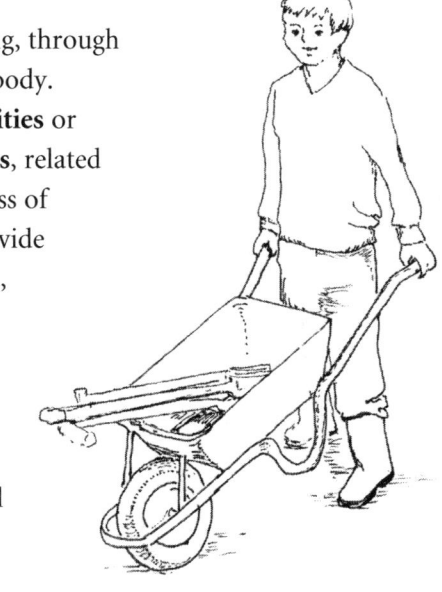

Developing good gross motor skills is necessary before children are able to develop fine motor skills. Giving a child a meaningful task, which achieves the same results as physiotherapy exercises, can give them motivation and encouragement to do more. For example, a young teenage lad with balance problems

Garden tasks can be great for developing gross motor skills

when walking, and little motivation to move at all, became transfixed with wheelbarrows and loved nothing more than wheeling a wheelbarrow around to collect leaves and take them to the **leaf mould** area. With a barrow in his hands he was happy to go anywhere, and he soon learnt to control it without help. Independence too!

In the garden there are numerous tasks that can help to develop fine motor skills too, such as seed sowing, '**potting on**' **plug plants**, **pruning**, taking **cuttings** or shredding herbs.

Improve self-confidence

Use practical activities with a positive outcome. For the more able pupils it is a chance to achieve a qualification with an emphasis on practical abilities rather than academic achievement. Sadly, too many children these days seem to lack self-confidence, especially if they are not strong academically. Schools, of necessity it seems, are increasingly focused on academic achievement. There are qualifications that young people can take which have an emphasis on achieving practical tasks rather than written work, for example City & Guilds or ASDAN. Making in-house certificates of achievement can also boost confidence and provide motivation.

It is important to know the child you are working with and to give them tasks that will suit their abilities and give them a sense of achievement. Young people can see that their skills, learnt through practical abilities, could give them a direction in which to go for further practical study or employment. Even without a qualification-based activity, children can see what they have achieved, and experience the satisfaction that comes with growing something yourself which others admire – or may even eat!

Provide some challenge

Create an environment, for those who are sufficiently aware, to introduce children to an element of risk. This benefit has to be weighed very carefully against health and safety considerations. However, in a garden situation it could provide children with the opportunity to use tools, carry heavy bags (if shown how to do so), wheel heavy loads and carry bricks. The key is to know your children and know the environment, and make a thorough risk assessment of activities.

Challenge can also be presented in the form of competition between individuals or teams, such as who can grow the heaviest potato harvest, sell the most bags of salad, produce the tastiest tomatoes or have the tidiest work bench. Again, know your children before presenting them with this kind of challenge.

Encourage awareness of the world around them

Give children an opportunity to be aware of the natural environment and of wildlife. This in turn can enhance and expand their world and provide opportunities for attention restoration in children who are very active, or agitated, physically and mentally. Some children may not be interested in plants, which do not move about, or may not respond immediately to stimuli. However, the wildlife in a garden can be a great source of interest, and this may be the way you entice them into the garden. It is also an opportunity to teach children about the importance of bees and butterflies, and the parts that woodlice and spiders play. They can admire spiders' webs and worm casts, watch birds feeding, listen to their song and be aware of different species.

Encourage awareness of the changes in the seasons and weather

By regularly walking around the garden and looking for weekly differences in the garden – the colour of leaves, flowers emerging and trees coming into leaf – we can help children to become aware of the effect of seasons, and explain why and how these changes occur. For those with the cognitive ability to understand, this is also a good opportunity to introduce basic biology in the 'outdoor' classroom.

Offer a place for sensory integration

A garden is an ideal place to stimulate the senses of children who are unable to go out and seek stimulus for themselves. In this way a garden can expand their world. By stimulating their senses, and thus their central nervous system, their ability to learn can improve. All gardens can be seen as 'sensory', but with careful planting and the addition of certain features (see Chapter 4) the overall sensory experience of being in a garden can be enhanced.

Enable some children to achieve a level of independence

Enabling some children to achieve a level of independence can be easier to achieve in a safe garden environment, with a consequent improvement in their self-esteem. Many children with SEND have regular support from teaching assistants and other carers. This enables them to access activities which would be otherwise too challenging for them, but it does mean that some can become very dependent on their carer.

Opportunities can be given in a garden environment where children can be 'left' safely to work independently under the watchful but hidden eye of support workers. The more open environment can offer children who are challenged by confined places and people the space they need to relax and function independently.

Encourage healthy eating habits

Gardening gives children the chance to grow and eat a range of foods they might not otherwise attempt. Through gardening they can learn about healthy eating, and have an understanding of where their food comes from. It is even better if gardening activities are linked with cooking, as children can see directly the connection between the two.

Give the chance to nurture

Giving a child the responsibility of caring for seedlings, cuttings or their own plot, or feeding the birds, also gives them the opportunity to learn how to care for, and improve the life of, other living things, whether they are plants or animals. This in turn can help them to be aware of their own needs and the needs of others.

Improve self-esteem

In addition to all of the above, gardening can give children who might otherwise be deemed as failures the chance to learn new skills. If they are then given the chance to share their skills or to support another child in a task, it can do wonders for their self-esteem. They may be able to earn in-house certificates of achievement or a practical-based qualification. It may be the first time in their school lives that this has happened.

Provide opportunities for employment and acceptance by society

Children who may struggle with basic academic skills, who may become disaffected with traditional schooling, may achieve with practical tasks and have their abilities recognised. This may ultimately lead to possibilities for future training and employment.

CHAPTER 1
Child-centred gardening

Meeting the *needs of the child* you are working with should determine the *task* you are doing with them. The needs of the *garden* should always come second, if you are using gardening to benefit the child.

Matching the task to the needs of the child

When choosing tasks, start from the child's strengths. By focusing on these, you can ensure that the child has a level of success, which can then boost confidence and encourage their participation in more challenging activities. By next selecting tasks on the basis of giving the child more of a challenge, you can develop their self-esteem.

Alternatively, you may be looking for ways of enhancing a child's experiences of the world, or to enable them to relax and reduce anxiety levels.

Many of the activities suggested below provide more than one benefit, so are mentioned in a number of categories. Ultimately the aim will be to give the child a degree of contentment, even happiness.

Tasks with physical challenge requiring a degree of upper body strength (gross motor skills)

Some of these tasks could be considered for children who need to increase their body strength or be encouraged to use their limbs. Activities can be used to augment other physiotherapy they receive, and provide them with meaningful tasks. Just taking a barrow from one place to another with a light load of leaves can give an uncoordinated child the opportunity to use both arms, to lift, move forward and steer, and do a useful job at the same time. Young people with plenty of (or too much!) energy can use this in a beneficial way and gain a positive feeling when they rise to the challenge. It can also improve their physical health.

Tasks could include:

- digging over ground-level beds and preparing beds for planting
- digging up potatoes or other crops (so rewarding!)
- barrowing and adding manure (which, contrary to their expectations, should not smell if it is well rotted) – *ensure that gloves are worn*

- digging holes for putting in posts and plant supports
- removing long-rooted **perennial** weeds, such as dandelions and dock
- digging out patches of perennial weeds and adding to a barrel to make 'nettle food'
- digging out large plants which need to be put undercover for the winter, or to remove unwanted shrubs or trees
- turning compost
- tidying leaf mould areas
- raking and sweeping leaves and other plant debris
- scrubbing paved areas clear of algae and other debris
- picking apples, using an apple picker for out-of-reach fruit
- pruning and sawing, such as **coppicing** trees
- collecting and barrowing **mulch** (e.g. bark chips), then raking it over the required area such as a path
- mowing using a powered lawnmower or a manual push mower
- moving plant material or tools from one place to another in a wheelbarrow
- sanding or scrubbing down wooden furniture to clean it or prior to adding preservative.

Meaningful tasks in the garden can help improve upper body strength

Tasks encouraging fine motor skills

Tasks can be used to help those with poor fine motor skills, or enable those who are well co-ordinated to demonstrate their strengths. There are also ways and means of helping those with poor fine motor skills to achieve some of these tasks:

- sowing 'seeds' – initially use bulbs, garlic or onions, then large seeds such as broad beans, conkers and acorns before going down the scale to pumpkins, sunflowers, marigolds, nasturtiums, beetroot or spinach
- tying up plants – use flexible wire to make this easier
- collecting seeds and transferring to containers – use large trays, funnels and containers with wide openings, and fill plastic bottles to make shakers
- writing labels using a DYMO® printer – large, horizontal labels make reading and writing easier, or use Garden and Horticulture label printers
- pruning shrubs – use ratchet pruners, which need less force to close
- picking flowers – use ratchet pruners, snips (small, scissor-like tools which may be easier to use than scissors for some) or adapted scissors
- making herb and lavender sachets (see Chapter 6)
- decorating terracotta pots with acrylic paints

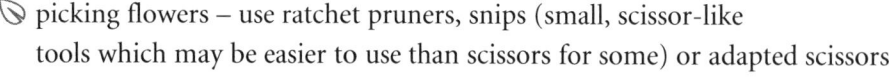

Sowing seeds

- potting on – use plug plants, or biodegradable cells in which to sow seeds, so the plant can be transferred to a bigger container easily (see Chapter 2)
- preparing fruit and vegetables for cooking – use knives, choppers or peelers
- grinding herbs and spices for cooking – use a pestle and mortar
- taking cuttings, snipping shoots, removing lower leaves (see Chapter 2)
- weeding with finger and thumb, to remove small weeds growing between more robust plants.

Tasks to encourage concentration

These tasks may include those children with an abundance of energy. If a child's concentration is poor, do tasks with a specific time limit and sandwich these between activities of their own choosing. You could also let them expend some energy before and after completing a task that requires them to be still and to concentrate. Select tasks that will not be too challenging if you want them to stick with it. Success can give encouragement. Those with a good focus, particularly if they have an obsessional nature, will love these tasks:

- observing and, if possible, recording wildlife (e.g. birds visiting the bird table, bees visiting flowers in a border, a spider building a web)
- making bird food or feeders
- planting seeds in rows (e.g. in a **raised bed**)
- writing labels for containers or beds
- planting up a small container
- collecting stones or broken pot pieces to put in the bottom of a large container
- going on a hunt for scented flowers, red leaves, stones with holes in, empty snail shells, and so on
- making a treasure hunt of mixed items to collect or look for
- sorting collections of gathered items (e.g. conkers, acorns, feathers, cones, leaves) into sets
- taking photos as a record of their plot through the year
- doing observational drawing or painting of flowers, seed heads and garden scenes.

Planting up a small container

Tasks providing opportunities for play

Giving young people the opportunity to play, messily if necessary and without restraint, not only provides a useful basis for all further learning, but also enables them to interact and communicate in a relaxed situation. Some children may need a little direction or some materials to be provided to initiate their play. Essentially it is a good opportunity, if at all possible depending on the needs of the child, for adults to stand well back.

Play opportunities could include:

- washing pots in warm soapy water and rinsing them afterwards
- sorting and stacking flowerpots into sizes, or using them to build a castle
- digging with tools – large or small – in an area of soil (where there are no plants growing) purely for the pleasure of digging, turning over and feeling the soil
- feeling the soil or compost with bare hands, and the addition of water when desired
- filling and emptying containers of all shapes and sizes with compost or water
- sieving soil
- creating a small fantasy or miniature garden from whatever they can find
- making camps in 'wild' areas from fallen wood
- cooking outdoors
- using berries and flowers to draw and paint with
- making music using found objects
- making masks or other art from found objects – these can be used to stimulate drama
- making constructions with wood or any found objects, with or without a purpose in view
- making and following trails
- playing hide and seek or 'chase' (if there is space)
- building scarecrows of their own design
- creating a story around the scarecrow figure, and using it in drama with a group, or making up words and music to fit the character.

Tasks to heighten sensory awareness – sensory integration

(This topic is considered in more detail in Chapter 5.)

Before embarking on activities to stimulate the senses, it is important to take into consideration those children whose sensitivities in some areas may already be very high. These hypersensitive children may react negatively to touch, sound, smell or taste and will not welcome activities which promote these. Instead, you may want to find opportunities to reduce their sensory overload (see opposite).

- Move around the garden with the child, identifying plants with an interesting feel, taste, smell or which make a sound, to stimulate those children unable to access these stimuli independently.
- Plant up a small container with plants for their sensory quality, for example herbs (smell, touch, taste), **succulents** (touch) or marigolds (taste and sight).
- Use swings, ropes or hammocks in the garden to stimulate the proprioceptive system of those needing this sensory stimulation.
- Collect items with different sensory properties (see Chapter 5).
- Provide containers of dry or wet soil or compost. Make sure it is not freezing cold

if fingers are very sensitive. Let the child put their hands in the soil, or help them to do so. Sprinkle soil onto their hands or feet. Discourage the use of tools, other than fingers and hands, to achieve the most benefit from this activity.

- Try walking in, or raking, leaves and listening to the sound.
- Lie on the ground or look up from a wheelchair, watch the movement and listen to the sound of leaves in the wind.
- Pick a bud and unfurl the new leaf.
- Pick up and scrunch dried leaves.
- Smell rotting leaves, and feel the warmth in a pile of them.
- Collect tree seeds (e.g. acorns, conkers and chestnuts).
- Learn about floating and sinking by putting tree seeds in a bowl of water – discover that those which float are not viable.
- Feel bark, hold a stick, hug a tree.
- Listen to the sound of birds in the trees.
- Observe wildlife.
- Tell a sensory story, preferably outdoors. Collect items from the garden to be used as part of the story.
- Walk along a barefoot path (see Chapter 4).

Playing in fallen leaves

How choosing the right tasks can help

Relaxing, allowing attention restoration, reducing sensory overload

When a child has high levels of anxiety, it can be caused by a whole myriad of reasons. Similarly, children who have been given a lot of direction may feel overloaded. If a child in your care is feeling this way, they are unlikely to be able to follow instructions properly or to learn. A garden environment is the ideal place to aid the 'attention restoration' they need. Here they can restore their equilibrium, clear their mind and settle their anxieties. This can be achieved by the 'soft fascination' of looking at their surroundings, sitting by a pond, or going for a walk over the soft grass, and smelling leaves and flowers.

Reducing sensory stimuli may also help. Giving them somewhere secluded from the sights and sounds of others can enable them to feel safe and calm.

- Create shelters with seats.
- Sit near a safe area of still water with a gentle fountain playing to soothe anxiety.
- Go for a walk round well-defined paths.
- Don't have any expectations of them 'achieving' anything. Use the garden as a space in which to 'chill'.

Getting rid of frustrations and anger

When a child is feeling very angry and/or frustrated, there is no point in trying to focus their mind on a task. They need to burn off the adrenalin before they can feel calm.

- Take them for a brisk walk.
- Allow them freedom to run in a wide-open space, if possible.
- Try some of the tasks with physical challenge requiring a degree of upper body strength (see earlier in this chapter), if you feel they are safe.

Encouraging confidence and self-esteem

Choose tasks that are within the child's capability, but at the same time may stretch them. Teach a task in small steps, so it does not appear too daunting at the start.

Sometimes it is beneficial to use **backward chaining**: learning a task by starting with the last step and moving backwards towards the initial step. Give the child the last stage of a task (the earlier steps having been completed by another individual or group), so that it is completed by them and they have the satisfaction of seeing a finished task. Once that is managed, then ask the child to do the last **two** steps, and so on. For instance, if the task is to **sow seeds**, start with the last step of watering and work backwards to the beginning:

9. Water the tray of seeds.
8. Label the tray of seeds.
7. Cover the seeds with a layer of sieved compost.
6. Sow the seeds.
5. Level the compost.
4. Overfill the tray with compost.
3. Break up compost in the tidy tray.
2. Collect scoops of compost from bags and put into the tidy tray.
1. Collect up all the equipment needed for the task.

Eventually it may be possible for a child to achieve each step, until they are able to complete the entire task *independently*. Finding tasks that a child can eventually do independently is a wonderful way to boost their confidence.

It is important for the child to realise that there has to be trust between you if you are to leave them to complete something on their own. For those who have always had assistance in school this can be very liberating, but you need to ensure that they are safe. Disengaged youngsters can really benefit and respond well, if they are trusted to do responsible jobs.

Issuing *certificates of achievement* for 'being a tidy worker', 'being helpful', 'growing the healthiest houseplant', 'growing the tallest hyacinth', or whatever you decide, can also encourage confidence. Use more regular rewards (e.g. for 'star gardener' of the day/session) too. Encourage the group, if they are able, to vote for the 'star gardener', giving their reasons. Reward badges and wristbands make effective regular rewards, which can be shown off to family and friends (see Sources of information). If it is possible for the children to achieve an accredited qualification such as ASDAN horticulture, that can do wonders for their self-esteem – and make their parents or carers proud.

Give them tasks which are reasonably assured of success, such as growing potatoes, pumpkins or runner beans. Let them be involved in the whole process, from sowing to harvest, so they can feel the sense of achievement. An element of competition can be introduced here – the longest bean, fattest pumpkin, ugliest vegetable, and so on – if your children thrive on this approach.

Give children their own plot or container to tend. Have a plot competition, if the children enjoy this. This helps them to learn the importance of nurturing for survival.

Give them a simple task which may involve social interaction, such as watering houseplants in the staff room, if this is where they lack confidence. Once they have mastered the task, with support, they may feel able to do it independently and then may feel able to show a less confident child how to do the activity too. This is guaranteed to boost self-esteem and confidence.

Similarly, give children in need of a confidence boost a job that is theirs alone – this will also give them a sense of responsibility (e.g. taking scraps to the compost heap, filling the bird feeders, tending the **wormery** or watering the seeds).

Encouraging social skills and interaction

There are opportunities to encourage interaction and improve social skills in many of the activities already described. For those children who struggle in these areas, particularly those on the autistic spectrum, you have to take things slowly. They may not want to join a group digging a bed in the field or sowing seeds around a table. Give them the space they need, let them be outside the group looking in (or sideways!) until they are comfortable, or settled with a task of their own. When they are ready, they may feel able to work just outside the group – or even with it, if it is a small one. Do what you can to help lower their anxiety levels. This may mean going for a brisk walk first. Use picture prompts rather than lots of words to direct and inform them (see Appendix B for examples of picture prompts).

Encourage small teams of children to work on one task, with each step being done by a different child. This can be a good way to introduce co-operation and interaction, but choose the children carefully!

Try to keep groups small. Large groups of children working on the same task can be a recipe for disaster. A child's needs can usually be met more successfully by working in small groups, with plenty of support if necessary.

If children are involved with gardening for several hours, then break times are another opportunity for socialising. Making refreshments and snacks for each other (as well as learning these skills) provides a good opportunity to nurture each other. It is also an excellent activity for wet weather. A meeting at the end of the session is equally effective and is a useful time to record activities, progress, likes and dislikes together.

A garden is an excellent place to sit and chat, share news and discoveries, have picnics and play, listen to stories or put on concerts, providing plenty of opportunities for interaction and co-operation.

Providing opportunities to gain qualifications and develop valuable workplace skills

This is particularly relevant to those young people who have become disengaged and school refusers, who cannot relate to the academic content of most secondary schools. A qualification based on learning and applying practical skills can build their confidence and self-esteem and give them a direction in which they feel they can participate and achieve.

Children with SEND can also achieve a qualification (e.g. ASDAN), which they might not otherwise get the opportunity to try.

Making tasks achievable

In order to make it possible for children with SEND to garden, adaptations may be needed in the choice of:

- task
- approach
- resources
- environment.

The task

Choosing the right task to suit the needs and preferences of the child is the best place to start when planning activities. If a task, such as seed sowing, seems beyond the abilities of a child with poor fine motor skills and little concentration, do not dismiss it as impossible. Consider the approach, the resources and environment.

The approach

- Could you help the child by using hand over hand, or hand under hand? (This may be recommended for children with PMLD.)
- Would the child find it easier if you worked alongside them?
- Could using picture prompts aid the child's understanding of what to do, and when?
- Could you give the child just part of the task to complete?

Perhaps they are able to crumble up the compost and fill trays for others to sow seeds in, or can they put the labels into completed trays of seeds? This idea of **backward chaining** (see also 'Encouraging confidence and self-esteem') – learning a task by starting with the last step and moving backwards towards the initial step – can be a more positive way of helping a child to learn a long process. By starting with the final step, they can have a sense of work completed.

Feeling the soil

The resources

- What resources might make the task more achievable?
- Are there any gadgets or devices which would make the task easier (e.g. a board with holes put over the seed tray (see Chapter 2), or a syringe to dispense the seeds, or seed tapes which can be placed in the seed tray)?
- Would it be better to use large seeds, such as broad beans, for the activity?
- Could you aid understanding by using picture prompts (see Appendix B) of the process before or during the activity?

The environment

- Would the child be better able to concentrate in a quiet environment on their own or in a small group?
- Would they find the reflections in a greenhouse disconcerting?
- Would they function better in a warm workroom than in a cold polytunnel?
- If the compost to be used is room temperature rather than cold and wet, would it be less off-putting?

It is worth mentioning here the view of **positive psychology**. In schools generally, the focus has been on children's weaknesses and ways of helping them to improve on these. If, instead, the focus is on what the child *can* do and activities chosen accordingly, this enables confidence and self-esteem to be developed. This positive approach, adopted by some schools, concentrates on nurturing the emotional wellbeing of the child in this way. Children may then be able to tackle more difficult tasks more effectively. In the garden context, it is often better to start with tasks the child *can* do, before tackling more challenging activities.

Managing a group

The most important resource that any teacher can have is support staff. When it comes to working with a group of children in a garden setting, the more staff the better. Although working as a team is a good aspiration and objective for children, it is not always the best one if other aims are to be achieved.

When children work as a group in the garden, they function differently to working one-to-one or two-to-one. Children may be unduly influenced and distracted by the behaviour of others around them. As a rule, working in smaller groups is more effective in achieving aims and objectives for individual children (unless 'working as a team' is the objective for that session).

Plan more than one activity, so that the group can be working in different areas of the garden or indoor space, and can be apportioned different tasks suited to their needs and abilities. This is where you need as many support staff as possible.

The whole group can come together for the beginning and end of a session to discuss what tasks are involved. At the end, the children can feed back as best they can what they have enjoyed, achieved or found difficult. This is an ideal opportunity to practise social skills, good listening and communicating.

As with any other lesson, a well-planned session is likely to be more successful than one hastily put together. Ensure that all tools and equipment are ready – unless, of course, that is part of the task you wish the group to carry out. Ensure that any support staff know what is expected of the children, and what the overall aims and objectives of the session are. Above all, *flexibility* is the key. There are so many variables involved, that you need to be able to adapt and alter ideas depending on the children and weather that day. It is a good idea to plan for a 'wet-weather alternative' to any outside activity. See Chapter 8 on year-round planning.

By considering all of the above when selecting a task to meet the needs of a child, there is more chance of them being able to relax and complete some – or all – of the task and to enjoy the experience. Success!

A sample session plan

The *aim* of your session is *what* you want your children to achieve; the *objectives* are *how* you are going to enable them to do this (i.e. the tasks they will do).

As an example, the session plan for FE students with SEND could look like the one opposite (also available on the CD-ROM).

A sample session plan

Date:	October
Group:	FE group A: James, Ali, Fozia, Jonas
Aim:	To improve self-esteem

Objectives:
Learning how to plant bulbs, decorate pots and planting for gardening gifts. Sowing seeds to enjoy in the summer and sell bunches of the flowers to give as gifts.

Session	Activities	Resources	Staff
9.30–12.00 *(Write here names of children to be assigned the different tasks)*	Group discussion and selecting tasks for the day. Warm-up activity (if necessary). 1 Sowing sweet peas 2 Planting crocus bulbs in pots 3 Decorating pots for bulb planting All activities can be done indoors or outdoors. 4 Tidying away and cleaning tools 5 Group discussion: show and communicate to the rest of the group what each has done	Personal protective equipment 1 Seeds, root trainers, compost, tidy trays, labels, pencils *(write here the children likely to do this task)*: **Jonas** 2 Bulbs, compost, tidy trays, labels, pencils: **James & Ali** 3 Terracotta pots, paints and brushes, water, labels: **Fozia**	*(Write here who is to work with which student)* **Peter** – work with James & Ali **Alison** – work with Fozia **Kristina** – work with Jonas

Outcomes:
Improved fine motor skills, independence, relaxation, improved focus, improved communication skills, heightened self-esteem, reinforced when gifts are made and received.

Notes for next session:
Use decorated pots for planting bulbs. Sow more sweet peas. Ali asked to do some pot decorating.

See Chapter 8 for a guide to seasonal tasks around the garden and other related activities. These are activities relevant to all gardeners, regardless of any special needs.

CHAPTER 2
Gardening: the basics

The activities described in this chapter are basic gardening and gardening-related activities. The size and nature of your garden or outside space, and the needs of your children, will determine which of these they could be involved in.

Growing flowers, vegetables, fruit, trees, shrubs and houseplants involves the following activities:

- seed sowing techniques and seed collecting
- pricking out and potting up – moving plants to a bigger growing space
- planting in the ground
- planting containers
- plant **propagation**, including taking cuttings
- feeding
- harvesting
- weeding
- mulching
- watering
- making compost and improving soil
- mowing grass (only students over 16 could participate in this, after some training)
- pest control
- pruning.

Garden maintenance tasks include:

- cleaning and sharpening tools
- washing pots
- repairing raised beds, fences and seats
- putting up supports
- tying in plants
- cleaning and maintaining furniture

- painting outside furniture, fences and other wooden structures
- sweeping and tidying paths, decking, patios and other paved areas
- coppicing.

Activities related to gardening include:

- encouraging wildlife
- caring for the environment, collecting rainwater, recycling
- preparing and eating harvested food.

Easy plants to sow and grow for beginners

The growing of plants begins with seed sowing, and this can be a very rewarding task with the potential for quick and successful results.

It may also seem rather daunting if you are working with children who have very challenging needs, as it can seem to be suited only to those with good fine motor skills. In fact, this is not the case, and there are many resources and methods you can use to make it possible for all children to participate in some way with the process.

1. Use large 'seeds', such as garlic cloves, onion sets or crocus bulbs. These are easier to handle than tiny seeds, and a child can still have the satisfaction of seeing something grow. If you want quick results, then try treated bulbs such as 'Paper white' narcissi in the autumn, which normally flower after six weeks (but be aware that these bulbs are poisonous).

2. Use seed tapes or mats, which are available commercially (although relatively expensive) or make your own with children who are capable (see Chapter 6). These are made from thin paper, in which seeds are embedded. Seed mats fit snugly onto a pot filled with compost. Even the most disabled children could be supported hand over hand to do this.

3. Fibre pots, rather than plastic ones, can be used. These will rot down in the soil eventually. Once the plant has germinated and grown, it can be potted on or put into its final growing space without the need to remove the pot (which can be problematical and can result in damaged plants).

4. Use Jiffy-7® pellets. These are small pellets filled with compost, which expand quickly when they are activiated in water (watching this happen can be a fascinating part of the lesson). Individual larger seeds can be placed in the top of one of these and it effectively becomes a small pot for the seed to grow in. As the seedling grows, the miniature plant can be potted on into a larger container with relative ease (see 'Potting on' on page 28).

5. Investigate the different sowing aids sold in garden centres, as they may work for you and your children. One which is effective is the short syringe with a spring. Staff can fill the container with small seeds and a child with poor understanding or poor muscle control could be supported to tap the syringe with their hand and release the seeds.

6. Sowing guides which rest on top of a seed tray (see 'Seed sowing' on page 24) can help those with visual impairment, or poor fine motor skills.

7 Mix tiny seeds, such as carrot, with sand – or glitter! This will make them easier to handle, you can see where they have been sown, and they can be sown more evenly. You can sow seeds straight into the raised bed or patch of ground where you want them to grow. Don't attempt this until the soil is warm enough in spring, because the seed won't germinate. Once you see tiny **annual** weed seedlings appearing in the soil, you will know that it is warm enough to germinate your seeds too. The soil will need to be thoroughly weeded and raked to make a fine seed bed before you do this. If you plant in marked rows, then anything germinating outside this line is likely to be a weed, so can be more easily removed. Young seedlings are susceptible to slug damage – the seedlings can literally disappear overnight! There is a better guarantee of success if seeds are started off indoors.

Plants for quick results

For quick results, try sowing:

- **micro-greens**
- salad – '**cut and come again**' mixed salad leaves
- radishes
- cress
- pea shoots.

Easy to grow

The following are easy, but take longer to germinate and harvest:

- spinach and Swiss chard
- beetroot
- leeks
- beans – broad, French and runners
- courgettes, marrows and pumpkins
- tomatoes
- peppers
- potatoes – sure of success!
- onions
- garlic
- crocus
- daffodils (harmful if eaten and a skin irritant) ☠
- hyacinths (harmful if eaten and a skin irritant) ☠
- tulips (harmful if eaten and a skin irritant). ☠

These flowers are easy to grow from seed:

- sunflowers
- marigolds (*Calendula*) (edible) 🍴
- poached egg plant
- cosmos
- godetia
- nigella (love-in-a-mist)
- pansies/violas (edible) 🍴
- borage (herb) (edible) 🍴
- nasturtium (edible) 🍴
- night-scented stock
- Californian poppy (*Eschscholzia*).

Basic gardening skills

Instruction sheets follow for some of the basic gardening skills. They can be photocopied and laminated and are also provided on the CD-ROM. The individual steps can be used as prompts to aid those capable of doing the task independently. Capable children could use these to put the process into the correct order after the
task has been done. This could also be part of an assessment process.

If you are new to gardening but keen to do some with your children, you could subscribe to a good gardening magazine for a year. Each month there will be advice on what to do and how to do it, with clear pictures. This way you can have useful visual prompts for you and the children, and help at hand to act as your guide and mentor.

Garden activity: Seed sowing (1)

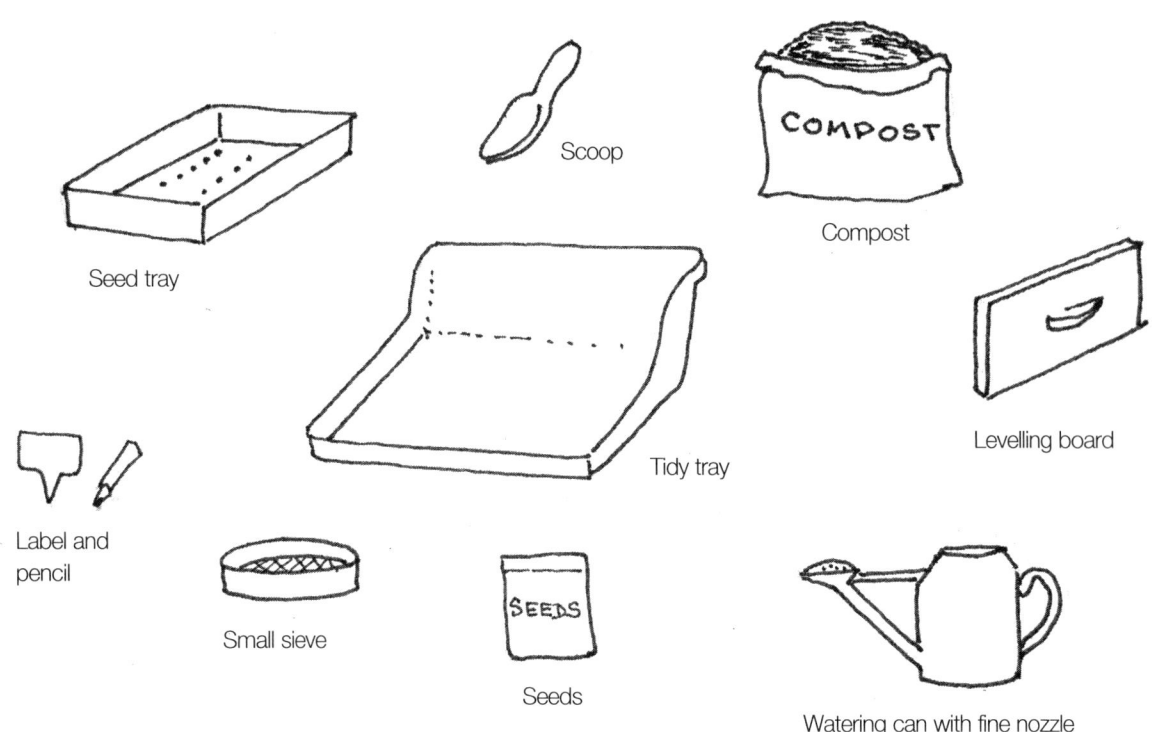

Equipment for seed sowing

Work in the 'tidy tray' or use an old tea tray or shallow cardboard box.

- Put sufficient scoops of compost into the 'tidy tray' to overfill a seed tray.
- Use hands to break up lumps in the compost.
- Use both hands to overfill the seed tray with compost.
- Level off the compost with the levelling board, using a sawing action.
- Tap the seed tray to consolidate the compost.

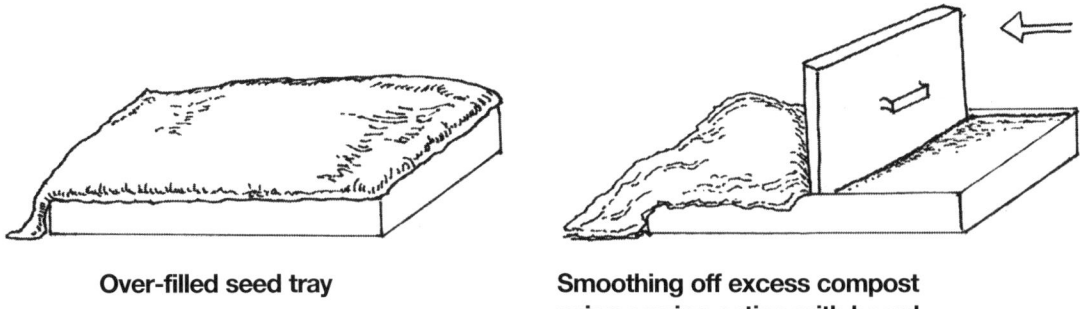

Over-filled seed tray

Smoothing off excess compost using sawing action with board

Garden activity: Seed sowing (2)

- Check sowing instructions on the seed packet regarding sowing distance. If helpful, use sowing aids such as hardboard or plywood boards (e.g. with lines drilled out, with small or large holes drilled out), which are made to fit over a seed tray and through which seeds are sown.

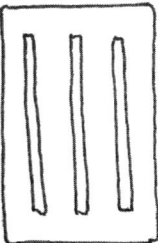 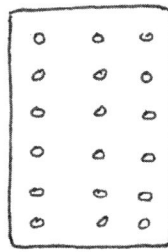 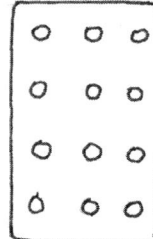

Sowing aids

These boards are particularly useful for those with poor fine motor skills, or with visual impairment. They can be made from hardboard or plywood using a jigsaw and drill. Other 'gadgets' are available from garden centres, but need to be tried out to judge their effectiveness for the children you are working with.

- Large seeds are generally sown at a depth of twice their size. Smaller seeds may be sown onto the compost surface and then covered with a layer of sieved compost.
- Label the seed tray.
- Water using the fine rose on a can, or by placing the seed tray in a large tray of shallow water. The latter is a safer method, as there is a danger of fine seeds being washed away by enthusiastic children using too much water.

The seed tray can then be placed in a polytunnel or greenhouse, or on a windowsill. Watch for germination.

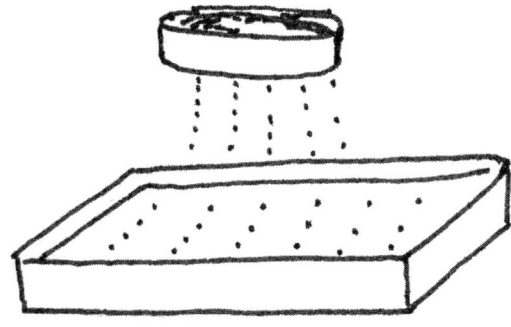 

Covering seeds with a fine layer of sieved compost   **Labelled seed tray**

Garden activity: Pricking out (1)

Equipment for pricking out

As soon as seeds can be handled, then it is time to move them to a larger growing space, usually a pot. This is known as **pricking out**.

If the seedlings are small, this can be a very delicate operation and not one for those with poor fine motor skills. There are aspects of the task they could participate in, though, such as filling the pots with compost, labelling or watering.

- Ensure that the tray of seedlings/cuttings has been well watered *before* pricking out.
- Working inside a tidy tray (or shallow box, tea tray or similar), fill a series of pots with well-crumbled compost. The compost used for seed sowing is suitable. As for seed sowing, overfill pots, scrape off the excess and tap the pot to settle the compost. This makes for good teamwork.

Pricking out the seedling

Garden activity: Pricking out (2)

- In the centre of the compost, make a roomy hole ready to receive the new seedling.
- Seedlings should only be held by their leaves. If the stem or roots are damaged by handling, the plant has no chance of survival. Holding the leaves, dig out the seedling using a pricking-out tool (e.g. the end of a teaspoon) or fork from the tray it is in, keeping the roots intact.

Placing the seedling in its new pot

- Carefully place the seedling into the ready-made hole in the pot. Gently firm in the seedling.
- Continue this process with all the seedlings.
- Label and water in.
- Place seedlings into a greenhouse, cold frame or sheltered spot, ready to be **hardened off**, and keep well watered.

This can be a time-consuming task, but it is soothing and therapeutic. Children's fingers are much smaller than adults', and the pricking out can be easier for them.

As for seed sowing, the whole process could be carried out by a team of children, each one assigned to a part of the task which they are best able to do.

Plug plants

Plug plants are small plants grown in plug-shaped cells of compost, sold at different stages of development, and available from garden centres or by mail order. They are not as cost-effective as seeds, but if you have limited time and space then they are ideal.

Buying them small, and potting them on as they get larger, can be cheaper than buying full-sized plants, and they are easier for the children to handle than small seedlings.

If, for example, you choose to have a mini-enterprise project, selling planted-up hanging baskets or other containers, then it would be a more cost-effective method to buy in plug plants early in the season and grow them on, rather than buying fully grown plants and using these.

Garden activity: Potting on (1)

Potting on is the process used when a plant outgrows its pot. A plant is put into the next-sized pot, so that its roots can continue to spread and allow the plant to grow. Therefore a plant which has outgrown a 9 cm diameter pot will then be potted on into a 13 cm diameter pot.

If you purchase **plug plants**, these will need to be potted on at least once before they are planted in their final position. Pricking out and potting on are ideal tasks when the weather is unsuitable for working outside, or if children need to be seated, as the tasks can be done indoors.

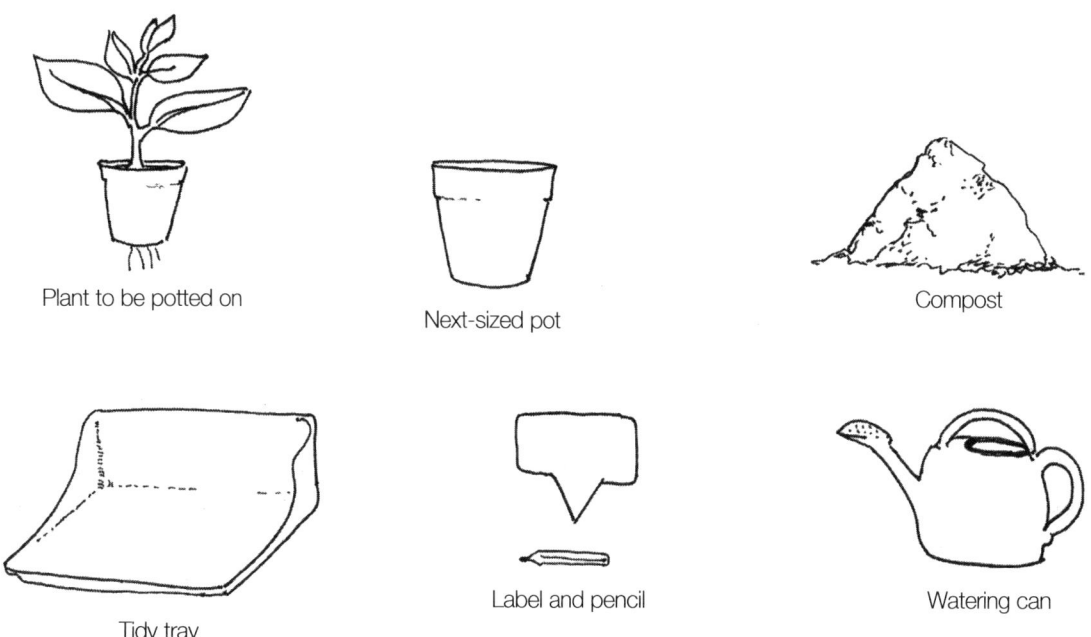

Equipment for potting on

- Plant to be potted on
- Next-sized pot
- Compost
- Tidy tray
- Label and pencil
- Watering can

❃ Working inside a tidy tray (or similar), break up the compost and put some into the bottom of the 13 cm pots that you are putting the plants in. Then place an empty 9 cm pot, the size the plant is already in, inside the larger pot. Continue to fill the larger pot, easing the compost round the edges of the smaller pot. Gently firm it in. It doesn't matter if compost also goes inside the inner pot, as it can be emptied out afterwards.

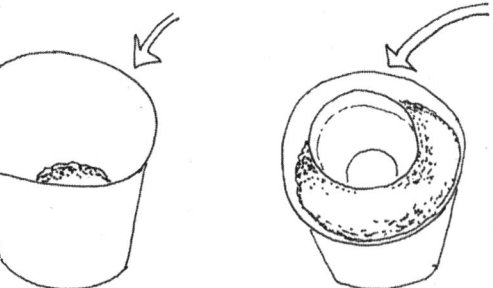

Preparing a bigger pot

Garden activity: Potting on (2)

- At this point, gently remove the inner pot. You now have a 'pot-shaped' hole in which to put your plant.

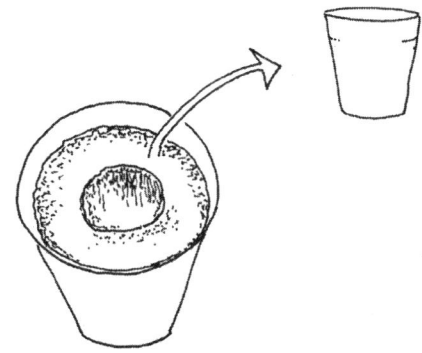

Removing the inner pot

- Carefully remove the plant to be potted on.

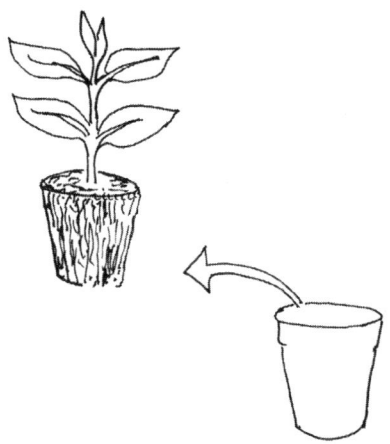

Removing the plant from its pot

- Then ease the plant into its ready-prepared space in the larger pot. Gently firm it into position and, if necessary, add a little more compost.
- Label, then water the plant.

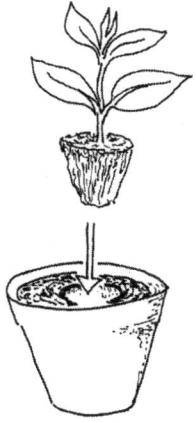

Placing the plant in its new pot

- This process can be repeated as necessary until the plant is sufficiently large to go into the garden or its final container.

© Becky Pinniger 2015 I *How to garden and grow: gardening as therapy for children with SEND* I LDA I Permission to photocopy

Garden activity: Planting in the ground, a raised bed or container

- Before starting to plant, make sure that the plants to be put in have been well watered. Anything in a pot should be soaked in water for an hour before planting, to ensure that the root ball is really moist.

- You may need to loosen the soil, using a border fork, in the area before you plant. If the area to be planted is small, such as a raised bed or container, a hand fork would be more suitable.

- Once the soil has been loosened, use the trowel if you are creating holes for smaller plants, and a spade to dig a hole for a tree or shrub.

- Make sure the hole is larger than the plant to be put in, to allow compost to be added to the hole first. A handful of bone-meal can also be added to the bottom of the hole for shrubs or trees before planting. This encourages development of a good root system.

- Once it is well soaked, carefully remove the plant from its container by tipping it upside down and tapping the bottom of the pot, carefully easing the plant as it comes out.

- Holding the base of the soil and root system, rather than the foliage of the plant, ease it into the prepared hole.

- Firm soil around the plant to ensure it is firmly in the ground. Water in well.

- Help plants to establish well by regular watering, particularly during dry spells. Supervise children – who generally *love* watering – or they may kill the plant with kindness by drowning it!

Planting in a raised bed

Garden activity: Taking cuttings (1)

Taking cuttings to make new plants involves using small shoots cut off from the stem of a parent plant. This process is straightforward, low cost and should have a reasonable success rate. The method described below encourages initiation and establishment of roots from the shoot.

This can be a very rewarding task and can increase your stock of plants very cheaply. Young plants can be used in the garden or sold as part of a mini-enterprise project. A few 'easy' plants will grow roots from cuttings simply placed in a container of water, for example mint, tomato, and *Tradescantia* (Wandering Jew) or *Chlorophytum* (Spider plant), which are grown as houseplants.

Part, if not all, of the process is achievable by all but the most severely disabled children. These children could benefit by working alongside someone making cuttings of herbs, such as rosemary, and enjoying the scent released by handling the shoots.

Softwood cuttings are taken during the spring at the start of the growing season, when the new growth on suitable plants is still soft, and not hard and woody. Herbs, such as thyme, lavender, rosemary, hyssop and marjoram, come into this category.

Semi-ripe cuttings can also be made during late summer and early autumn, when the stem has partially hardened and is becoming woody.

Hardwood cuttings are made from leafless dormant woody stems of **deciduous** plants, such as Dogwood (*Cornus*).

❋ Choose shoots that are 7–10 cm long, without flowers or buds. As soon as they are cut from the parent, place the cuttings in a bucket of water or a plastic bag, to reduce water loss. Preferably take cuttings in the morning, and keep them in the shade until ready to use.

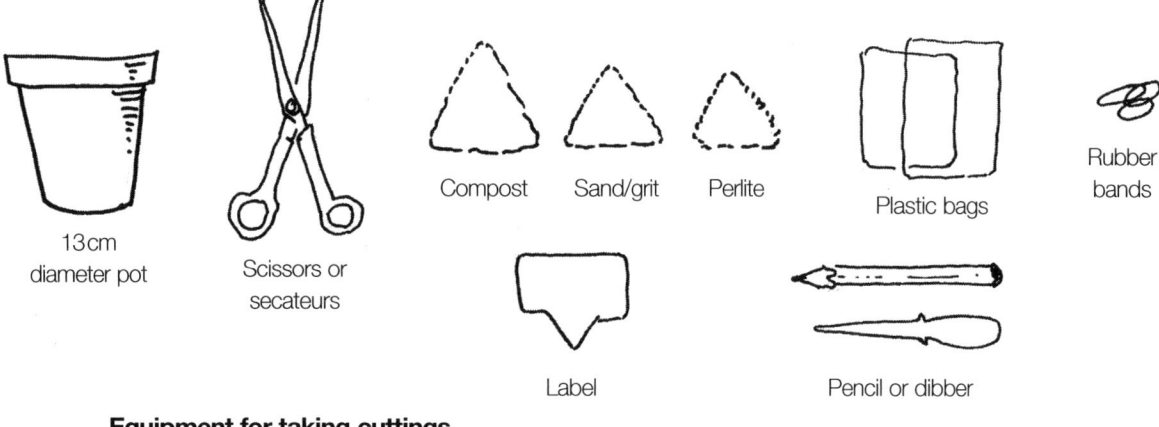

Equipment for taking cuttings

Plant propagation can be done in many ways, including by sowing seeds and bulbs, and by making cuttings. More information can be found on the Royal Horticultural Society website or in any good gardening manual.

Garden activity: Taking cuttings (2)

- Cut just below the **node**.
- Take off the leaves in the lower part of the cutting. This will reduce water loss by the shoot while roots are forming.
- Mix the compost and grit or **perlite** together. The addition of grit and perlite opens up the texture of the compost, ensuring that there is good drainage and less likelihood of the cuttings rotting. Seed and cutting compost can be used in preference to ordinary multi-purpose compost. Fill a 13 cm diameter pot with the mixture.

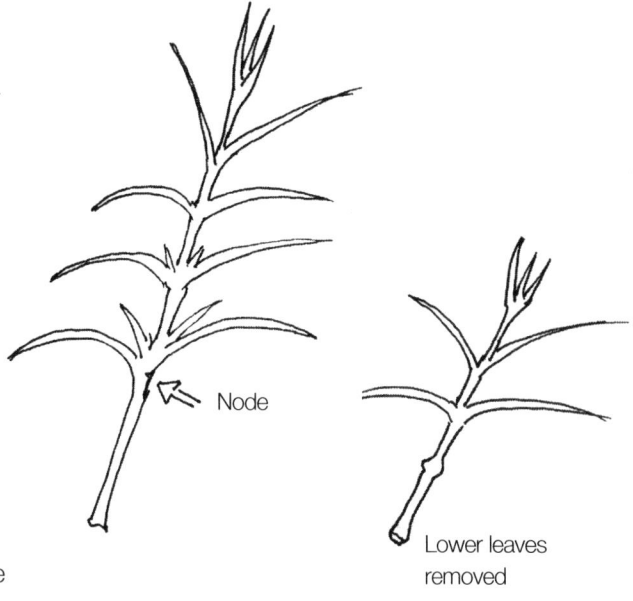

Taking cuttings

- Make holes around the pot edge with a pencil or the end of a plastic fork. Insert cuttings one at a time into the holes and firm in. Leaves should not be in contact with the compost, or they will rot. Water from above and label the pot.
- To reduce water loss, the pot can be covered with a plastic bag (secured with a rubber band) – or an old shower cap! Cuttings need to be encouraged to develop roots as quickly as possible, so that the plant's small food reserve is not exhausted. The cuttings should be exposed to the variables of the weather as little as possible. Ideally, put cuttings into a polytunnel or **cold frame**, out of direct sun.

Fill pot with compost and perlite mix

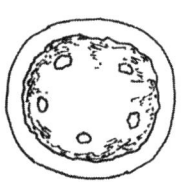

View from above showing holes in compost

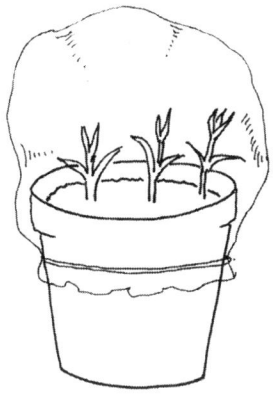

Cuttings covered with a plastic bag

Placing cuttings in a pot

*Check on the seedlings regularly, and after a few weeks very gently pull those that look as if they are growing. If there is some resistance, it suggests that roots have formed. Leave the cuttings in the pot until it looks as if new leaves are forming. That is the time for them to be **potted on** (see 'Potting on' on page 28).*

Garden activity: Feeding plants

Container-grown plants

Plants grown in containers have a limited source of nutrition, so will need to have liquid or granular food added to the compost when they are planted. After six weeks this is used up and weekly feeding with a proprietary liquid food is necessary. This is the case for summer-flowering plants. There is less need to feed plants during the dormant winter season.

Making your own plant food

Alternatively, make your own liquid feed by collecting leaves from comfrey plants (which grow wild in damp shade) and/or nettles. If you have space, it is worth cultivating comfrey plants and using a shady damp area for them to grow in and be regularly harvested for plant food.

The leaves are chopped up and put in a lidded container, covered in water, and left in a shady spot. After about six weeks, pour off the concentrated dark liquid and store in old milk bottles or similar (clearly labelled). The concentrated liquid should be diluted with water 1:20 and used to encourage fruit and flower production.

 Warning: it smells horrible!

Feeding established plants in beds

Well-established plants grown in the ground do not have such immediate needs. If an area is to be newly planted, prepare the soil first by adding an organic fertiliser such as 'blood, fish and bone' or pelleted chicken manure. This is scattered over the area to be planted and forked in prior to planting, to encourage healthy growth. This can be done during the autumn and winter.

Garden activity: Harvesting

This is the fun part of the whole growing process, when children can reap the rewards of their hard work.

Equipment

This will depend on the food being harvested.

You will need:

- a clean container, for example a bucket for potatoes or a small food carton for salad or raspberries
- a large or small fork, scissors for salad crops, beans or spinach, and nimble fingers for juicy fruit and peas.

If anyone is at all reluctant about gardening and is physically capable, then suggest they dig up one or two potato plants (mid- to late summer). It never fails to amaze and surprise them how one potato can produce so many.

Potatoes grown in pots can be harvested even by those who are wheelchair dependent. Bags can be placed near them and the child guided to feel in the compost and produce (hopefully!) small round edible 'gold'. Washed and cooked, served with a little butter and some chopped parsley from the garden, they can be eaten at any time and are delicious.

Harvesting other produce may involve more fine motor skills: snipping lettuce leaves, pulling out radishes, snipping spinach or chard, gently pulling tomatoes from the plant, picking and podding peas. Raspberries, currants and strawberries can be immediately rewarding, although it is good practice to encourage washing of all harvested produce. Again, having produce growing in containers or in raised beds can enable all children to participate in some harvesting, even if they need hand-over-hand support.

Harvesting provides an opportunity to talk about colour, size and shape before, of course, discussing taste. Teach the children how to tell when a tomato is ripe, or which part of the 'cut and come again' lettuce to pick (not the small, central leaves).

Washing and preparing food for eating is also part of the process and can be an enjoyable sensory experience. Encourage children who can, to eat some of the washed fruit or vegetables raw (e.g. tomatoes, peas, carrots, grated beetroot). They are sweeter and full of vitamins then. Broad beans picked young are very tasty raw – unlike the bitter taste of old beans picked past their best and boiled to death, which puts many people off eating them.

Garden activity: Weeding (1)

Inexperienced gardeners sometimes worry about weeding. What is a weed? What is a wild flower? Essentially a weed is any plant which you don't want, growing in your flower or vegetable patch. Very often they are plants which grow in the wild, so are essentially wild flowers, but can be so prolific as to be a nuisance in the cultivated part of a garden.

Annual weeds are the smaller plants growing between your vegetables or cultivated flowers. If you leave them and let them set seed, then you will be multiplying the problem. Weeds take water and nutrients from your cultivated plants, and may even overtake and choke them.

Weeding

Equipment

This will depend on the size of the weeds and the place where the weeds are growing. It could include:

- large or medium border fork – for large, long-rooted perennial weeds
- small hand fork for smaller annual weeds
- hoe
- bucket or trug for weeds
- kneeling mat or stool.

Hoeing

Hoes are good tools to use if the ground is dry, and you can get between the cultivated plants. The weeds are chopped off as you hoe and, if it is dry weather, can be left to wither on the bed. If there is any chance of rain, then the weeds need to be picked up and put on the compost heap.

Anyone using a hoe has to have good co-ordination and stability when standing – it is not the easiest of tasks, but is not as physically demanding as digging with a border fork.

Garden activity: Weeding (2)

Hand weeding

Hand weeding (kneeling on a mat if the bed is not raised) using a small trowel or fork requires fine motor skills and an ability to discriminate which plants are the weeds. Again, this task will not suit everyone.

To make the task easier for those unable to discriminate between plants to be kept and those to be removed, place flowerpots over the plants to be kept. Anything uncovered is to be removed. This is a good method to use in a raised bed, when children have to pass a 'weeding assessment' for some qualifications. Weeding *can* be very rewarding, but it may be too open-ended and fiddly a task to be given to anyone hyperactive or needing clear boundaries.

Removing perennial weeds

For the physically fit, weeding an area with large *perennial weeds* (e.g. dandelion, dock, couch grass, thistle, bindweed and nettle) can be rewarding and can use up lots of energy. These plants will survive for at least two years in soil if left, and if they re-seed, can be with you forever! Perennials do die down in winter, but come up in spring unless removed. If even a small piece of the root is left in the soil, it can regenerate, so their challenge is to get the whole root out – no easy task as they can be extremely long!

Others, such as couch grass, have long but shallow roots running in all directions under the soil and are equally hard to remove. These weeds should not be put on the compost heap, as they will not be killed by the relatively low temperature achieved in the average garden compost heap. Instead, put them in a council green bin, if possible, or in a skip.

Nettles can be kept. If you have the time and space, you can put them to rot in a black bin, and use the liquid obtained to feed your plants (see 'Feeding plants' on page 33). Whoever does this task needs to wear thick gloves and ensure that arms and legs are well covered.

Mulching

Prevention is better than cure, so you can try mulching (see 'Mulching' opposite) to reduce the amount of weeding you need to do in the garden.

Garden activity: Mulching

Mulching is the process of covering bare soil, usually with one of the following:

- compost
- wood chips
- pebbles
- grit
- slate chips.

Mulching is done for various reasons, but it basically ensures that evaporation of moisture from the soil is reduced, weeds are suppressed, and the appearance of the plants in the bed or container is enhanced. If you are using compost as mulch, then this will also improve the condition of the soil.

You will need:

- one of the above mulching materials
- shovels or spades
- barrow or small trug
- rake, hand rake or fork (depending on the size of the area to be mulched).

Grit is used around alpine plants, because they are particularly susceptible to the wet, and this reduces the chances of them rotting when conditions are wetter than they are used to in their native habitat.

If you are choosing to mulch a planted area, do so once it has been weeded, and water the plants well before applying the mulch. The mulch will then help to retain the moisture, which is important in hot summer weather.

Mulching using wood chips is usually done to make paths. **Weed-suppressant membrane** can be placed along the path, pegged down and then covered in a thick layer of wood chips. This will suppress weeds and make garden maintenance easier. Shovelling, barrowing and spreading bark mulch makes an excellent activity for energetic and enthusiastic youngsters during the colder months.

You may be able to find a local supplier of wood chips, for example your local council, who may provide it free of charge.

It is recommended that you only add wood chips to cultivated areas with mature trees or shrubs growing. Nitrogen can be leached from the soil as the wood chips slowly rot, and this would be detrimental to the growth of new or young plants.

If you are mulching paths with wood chips, it can be done at any time of the year. If adding it as a weed suppressant or to hold in water, spring and autumn are the best times of year to do so.

Barrowing and spreading mulch is an excellent job for the physically fit, and those with a lot of energy. It is a good way to expend energy, keep warm and work as a team. Those who are less physically able could be supported to do some spreading, or adding of mulch around plants in pots, small or large.

Garden activity: Watering

Children *love* watering, particularly in warm weather.

You will need:

 hose, sprinkler or watering cans

 water from a tap or water butt.

Newly sown seeds or small seedlings can be watered by placing the containers in trays of water, which will soak into the pot. Otherwise it is all too easy for them to be washed away by overenthusiastic watering with a can with large holes, or which drips.

Small plants can be watered using a can with fine holes, or a hose with a fine spray attachment. There are small nozzles which can be screwed onto drinks bottles to make good waterers, which do not release too much water at once. They do need some strength to use, however, and two hands to squeeze the bottle. They are ideal for individually potted plants or new seedlings.

Larger plants can be watered using a watering can rose with larger holes (or no rose at all), as long as the water is directed at the *roots*, which are the part of the plant taking up the water.

It is best to water at the earliest or latest opportunity during the day, to reduce the amount of water that evaporates. Water thoroughly once or twice a week rather than a small sprinkling every day, which encourages roots to come to the soil surface rather than grow deep into the ground.

If a child is particularly keen on watering and it is the one and only task they will do, then find a tree or other well established plant that will not 'drown' easily, which they can water freely.

Those young people who are able to do so, can learn the whole process of attaching a hose to a tap, turning it on and directing the water – and the advantages of the different types of spray on a nozzle. Winding up the hose when you have finished is also part of the task.

By using different types of watering implements, the task can be made accessible for most children, whatever their specific needs.

 Important: ensure that water butts are safe for the children you work with. Use them to fill cans for watering outside, and to teach the importance of recycling.

Garden activity: Making a compost heap (1)

Ideally, every garden should have its own compost heap, into which waste can be recycled to make compost to add to the soil to improve it. If space is limited, then consider having a wormery instead.

From the children's point of view a compost heap is a good facility to have, because it is:

- a perfect demonstration of the benefits of recycling
- a good example of how something can change over time
- an ideal opportunity to observe and be aware of small creatures and microorganisms
- an opportunity for some 'heavy work' – turning compost, barrowing and spreading compost
- an opportunity for smaller-scale activities – shredding paper, collecting waste, snapping twigs to put in and sieving compost to be used.

Compost containers can sometimes be obtained free from local councils, and consist of a plastic barrel with a lid. They are also available in a variety of guises in garden centres and DIY shops. Others can be constructed using discarded wooden pallets or old scaffolding boards.

Ideally, compost heaps should hold some warmth and moisture, enable drainage and let in air. Place them where they will not be subjected to extremes of temperature, preferably in partial or full shade. If the base is placed over soil, then there are soil organisms ready to be included in the heap. If you build over a stone base, then add some soil to the bin to incorporate some soil organisms so that the rotting process can begin.

What can be composted?

Compost heaps need to contain about 25–50 per cent green (nitrogenous) waste, such as grass cuttings, annual weeds, fruit and vegetable waste (uncooked). Used coffee grounds (often available free from coffee shops) are an excellent source of nitrogen too; and can also be used as a mulch around plants to add nutrition and may deter slugs at the same time.

Some 50–75 per cent of the heap should consist of brown (carbon) material, such as paper, cardboard, wood chippings, straw and woody stems.

It is important to ensure that there is a good balance in the heap, and not too much of either brown or green material. Grass cuttings are particularly prone to going slimy and smelly if they are not regularly mixed with a proportion of brown waste.

Shredding card and paper for the compost heap can be a good task for some children.

Turning the heap, which helps speed up the process of rotting, can be good hard work, and provides an excellent opportunity for examining the tiny worms and other organisms inhabiting the heap.

The heap can also be watered during dry spells to ensure it stays moist.

By having more than one heap, the compost can be turned from one container to the other. The whole rotting process can be fascinating for children.

Garden activity: Making a compost heap (2)

☠ Children who may put their hands in their mouths, eat anything within their reach, or who have allergies to mould and spores, should not be involved in making or using compost.

Once the compost is dark brown and no longer resembles its separate components, it will be ready to use. It will not be as even in texture as that purchased in garden centres; however, its condition can be improved by sieving. Construct or purchase a large sieve to be held over a wheelbarrow, and involve the children in the sieving process, which can be warm work and rewarding. Large pieces can be returned to the heap for further rotting.

It is likely that if you add annual weeds to your heap, then their seeds will not be destroyed in the rotting process, which in a small heap (such as a school or home garden) will not get sufficiently hot to cause this to happen. You may find you have a rash of weed seedlings added to your bed as a result, but they will be annuals and easily removed.

Do not compost perennial weeds, such as nettle, dandelion, dock, bindweed, couch grass, horsetail or thistle.

Do not add the roots or seed heads of these weeds to a compost heap or they will return to haunt you! If you have the facility, recycle these in a council garden waste bin, where they will be rotted down and the compost sterilised.

Garden activity: Pest and disease control

Pests are part of the wildlife of your garden area.

If greenfly or blackfly are eating your beans, then put in plants to encourage ladybirds, whose larvae will enjoy eating them. It is a good opportunity to help children understand about the balance in nature and the importance of helping to maintain this. Nowadays there are several biological controls available.

One group of pests is able to ravage plants quicker than you can deter them: slugs and snails. There are plenty of ways of trapping them, or using barriers which will not involve chemicals. This could make a good basis for a science project!

A good source of further information is the RHS Campaign for School Gardening website: https://schoolgardening.rhs.org.uk/home.

Garden activity: Pruning

Plants are pruned in order to:

- keep them from outgrowing their space or losing their shape
- encourage flowering/fruiting.

The subject can seem very confusing, but a good tip is: prune spring-flowering shrubs immediately after they have flowered, if you want to ensure blossom for the following year. If you cut back in summer, then you may remove the very stems bearing the buds for flowers next spring.

When you cut a stem, cut at an angle just above a leaf bud. If you cut in the middle of a stem, then the rest of the stem will die back to the bud.

For pruning specific plants, it is best to refer to the RHS website (www.rhs.org.uk/) for clear information.

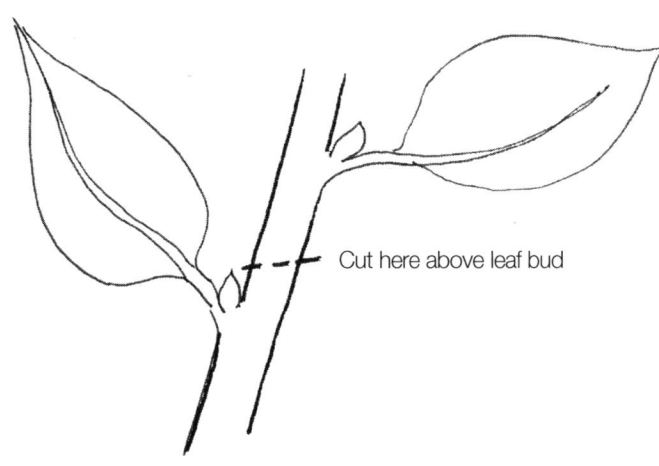

Cut here above leaf bud

Pruning

CHAPTER 3
What to keep in your 'shed'

Tools and equipment

It is worth investing in proper well-made tools if your school is committed to the benefits of horticultural therapy, and in maintaining the school garden. Nowadays there are good 'child-sized' or 'apprentice'-sized tools, which are ideal for smaller individuals who would not have the strength to manage an adult-sized equivalent. Do not be tempted to buy brightly coloured, less robust, 'children's tools', which are best kept for a sandy beach.

Ideally, before purchasing any tools, test them out first for:

- weight
- size
- grip
- balance.

Small children, or those with limited strength, will benefit from lighter tools that are easy to grip. The lightest available tools are made from plastic, aluminium or carbon fibre.

Stainless steel is easy to maintain, and forged steel is the strongest. If you work with physically fit teenagers, these may be the best choice.

Listed in the table opposite are some basic tools. You may not need all of these, as it will depend on the nature and size of your children and garden. In the second column are some alternative suggestions.

Tool	Alternative suggestions
Hand trowel (often called 'spades' by children)	Strong spoons of varied sizes.
Hand fork	
Digging spade	Use purpose-made children's tools of good quality.
Border fork	Use purpose-made children's tools of good quality.
Tidy tray	Tea tray or a cut-down strong cardboard box.
Watering can	Plastic bottles and purchased spray top.
Small sieve	Plastic food container with a vegetable net bag.
Seed-sowing gadgets	If they work for you, try folded pieces of card, pepper pots, home-made seed tapes, etc. (see Chapter 6).
Storage container for seed packets	Cardboard box covered in collage of seed packets, cut-outs from seed catalogues, etc.
Leaf rake	Use purpose-made children's tools of good quality.
Wheelbarrow	Choose carefully to ensure that it is strong, easy to handle and not too heavy. Alternatively, a child's trolley or shopping trolley (for some lighter loads).
Labels for pots/containers	Wooden stirrers, wooden cutlery, lolly sticks, a fly swat, laminated seed packets, driftwood with pokerwork names (i.e. using a tool similar to a soldering iron to 'burn' letters into wood, although there may be health and safety considerations), DYMO machines, etc. (see Chapter 6).
Gloves	Buy good quality ones, pegs to keep together and name labels. Use a cheap sock hanger to hang up to dry and store.
Seed and plant containers – flowerpots, seed trays	Re-use food and drink containers. Those with clear plastic tops make good 'mini-greenhouses'. Make biodegradable pots from recycled paper (see Chapter 6).
Compost (often called 'dirt' by children and uninitiated staff)	Make your own in a compost heap (see Chapter 2), sieve before use. This is *not* an alternative to purchased compost for sowing seeds.
Large and small pruners	If possible, buy good-quality pruners to last, but if funds are low, cheaper ones will do. Avoid the cheapest '£1 shop' tools, which are often useless!
Cloth for cleaning sharp tools	Use an oily rag kept in a plastic bag, or cloth hand mop, and wipe over secateurs rather than washing them.
Bucket, tub-trug or large container to hold water safely and for washing tools after use	Old washing-up bowl or a plastic box.
Brush for cleaning tools and a cloth to wipe them dry	Use worn out washing-up brushes, and old towels for drying.
Clothes for wet and cold weather	Search for boots and woolly hats in charity shops.

The following pieces of equipment are not essential, but can broaden children's understanding of the natural environment:

- a wormery – instructions on how to make your own can be found on the internet
- a cold frame – in which to keep tender plants or seedlings that are not ready to go outside, and for growing salad crops early or late in the season; use polystyrene boxes formerly used for packing fish or chilled goods, and add a lid with a piece of Perspex.

Adapted tools for children with SEND

Add-on grips can be purchased to add to tools and reduce hand, wrist and arm strain. See, for example, www.activehands.com

Tools from Peta (UK) Ltd (www.peta-uk.com) also provide add-on handles, which can be fixed to standard gardening tools. These can improve grip.

Digging can be aided by using hand tools with an upright handle, available from some garden centres. Long-handled hand tools may be easier to use than large digging tools, and better suited to wheelchair users.

Weeding with a hoe is a skill to be learnt, and may be beyond some children, although child-sized hoes are available. Some manufacturers sell different-length handles to which various tool heads can be attached. These may be suitable if you work with children of differing sizes and strengths.

Raking is also a hard technique for some, who may try to dig with the rake rather than gently skimming backwards and forwards over the soil surface to reduce lumps. A fist-grip style of handle and cuff is available from Peta (UK) Ltd, to make the rake easier to use.

Similarly, sweeping can be made easier. Sweepings can be moved to a large plastic sheet, which can be emptied onto a compost heap if the traditional dustpan and brush is too difficult.

There are several 'aids' to make the task of seed-sowing less fiddly, but you need to try them out to see how easy you find them to use first. (See suggestions in Chapter 6.)

More information about adapted tools is available on the internet, including on the Thrive website: www.thrive.org.uk or www.carryongardening.org.uk.

Protecting hands and feet

Footwear and gloves are also an important consideration.

Steel-capped boots or wellingtons are best for those able to participate in active gardening, but sturdy shoes may suffice if these are not available. Encourage staff to take the same precautions.

Gloves come in all shapes, sizes and fabrics – look for those which provide protection if heavy work or thorns are to be tackled. Otherwise, there are gloves which fit closely to enable finer work to be carried out, while still preventing hands from getting dirty. Wearing gloves can be problematic for those with sensory issues, but so can touching compost with bare hands. It is best not to have hard-and-fast rules, but to encourage use of gloves with anything likely to damage the skin, such as pruning spiky bushes or removing nettles. Keep gloves hanging up if possible (pairs pegged together), or in a box. Wash fabric ones frequently; putting on gloves caked with a layer of

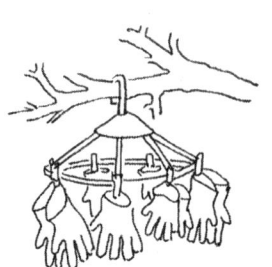

Sock hanger used for gloves

dry soil is not comfortable or encouraging.

Lots of warm soapy water will be needed for washing hands at the end of each session, whether or not gloves have been worn.

Using tools

Children, and some staff, will need to be shown how to hold and use tools efficiently and effectively; it is a skill to be learnt. For example, unless children are shown how to insert a trowel into the soil and carefully remove it to make a hole, there is a tendency to flick soil in the air with it. Also, injuries to backs can develop if larger tools are not held and used correctly. Children may tend to push a tool in with their stomach, rather than having their back straight and using their foot to push the edge of the tool into the soil.

For detailed information and advice on how to use and care for tools, look at the RHS website and Campaign for School Gardening (https://schoolgardening.rhs.org.uk/home), which includes health and safety.

Make care of tools a part of your gardening session. If possible, have children involved in:

- getting their own tools (or for the group) from the tool store
- collecting tools up at the end of the session
- cleaning and drying the tools
- putting back the tools in their correct place.

To make this part of the session, ensure that tools are kept safely and in labelled areas. This encourages literacy and shape recognition. It also provides:

- opportunities for teamwork
- an opportunity to learn about care of tools
- an awareness of safety issues.

Taking care of your tools

Useful sources of equipment

Charity shops and jumble sales are a good source of 'equipment' – others can be 'recycled' from everyday items such as food packaging. You will also need plastic boxes – and somewhere to store them!

Here are some other ideas:

- China containers can be used for planting bulbs for presents. Ensure that there are crocks in the bottom and use bulb fibre to ensure good drainage.
- Small baskets, preferably lined with plastic, can be used for flower arrangements or planting bulbs.
- Anything which can hold soil and from which water would not run out too quickly, but does have some sort of hole for drainage, can be adapted and used as a 'fun container' for plants – colanders, old wellingtons, workers' safety helmets

Recycled containers

or boots, shopping baskets, wooden boxes, old wooden drawers. Other containers, such as teapots, can be used to hold plastic plant pots.

- Cutlery, metal, wood or plastic can be used as alternatives for small hand tools.
- Warm and wet weather clothing, such as boots and hats, can enable gardening in all weathers.
- Books on wildlife, plants and gardening provide a useful resource for research and discussion.
- Containers for seed packets, such as tins and plastic boxes, provide a means for storing and sorting seeds.
- Jars are usable as containers for home-made preserves.
- Plastic toys and containers are good for using with water and for soil play.
- Small plastic figures or animals can be buried in soil beds used for digging in, and used with miniature gardens.
- Children's trolleys can be used for transporting items such as plastic flower pots.
- Shopping baskets on wheels, which are often readily available to buy second-hand, can be used for transporting compost and tools to their destination.
- Anything adaptable can be used for plant labels, for example a fly swatter (nice and large for those with visual impairment), plastic cutlery, old hand tools which can be brightly painted and used as more permanent labels.

Planted-up old work boot

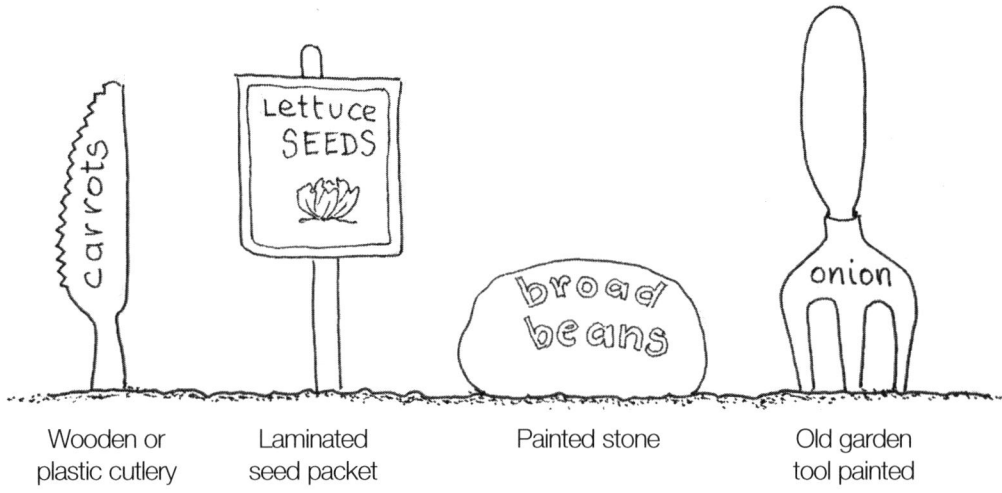

Different ways of labelling using recycled materials

Wooden or plastic cutlery · Laminated seed packet · Painted stone · Old garden tool painted

- Use unwanted terracotta flowerpots to decorate for bulb planting and other presents.
- Stack up old tyres as a planter for potatoes. They can be painted before planting.

Reuse old tyres as a potato planter

- Recycle washed food containers of all shapes, sizes and materials. Drainage holes may need to be added. Keep transparent lids, as these can be used to make mini-greenhouses for germinating seeds.

  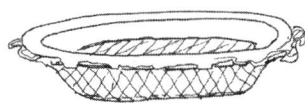

Old drinks containers and lids make ideal propagators   **Reuse wooden cutlery**   **Recycle fruit net bags and containers to make sieves**

- Keep washed drink containers, with lids if possible.
- Save unused wooden stirrers, lollipop sticks, wooden cutlery (offered in some cafes).
- Use wool, string and raffia for tying up plants and for craft activities.
- Recycle vegetable and fruit net bags to make sieves.

Garden centres and suppliers may be happy to donate equipment or provide it at a reduced price if you give them some publicity – in your school magazine, for example. Some supermarkets operate a voucher system, enabling you to exchange them for equipment.

Somewhere safe to hold your tools is equally important. If they are not easily accessible and are kept in a muddle in boxes in a cupboard, unwashed after each use, people will feel less inclined to go out and garden. Ideally, a small shed or tool store is the answer and may not be difficult to find free or second-hand on the internet.

Choose tools carefully to make gardening as easy, safe and enjoyable as possible, so that everyone can reap the benefits of working in the garden.

CHAPTER 4
Garden design considerations

When designing a garden to be used by children with SEND, their specific needs should be considered. It is also important to determine whether the space is for children to enjoy *being* in, or is it somewhere for the children to *participate* in gardening? Ideally, gardens can provide both.

All living things need sun to grow and thrive, and this includes children. Consider the orientation of the garden space so the plants and people involved can benefit. Although the garden will need a sunny site, if the children are to gain maximum use from their garden there will need to be some shelter from extreme weather conditions. Arbours and permanent awnings can provide this, and an indoor working space such as a polytunnel is ideal in poor weather. If the children are healthy, then poor weather doesn't have to mean they stay indoors. With the right clothing, children can be outside whatever the weather! Ideally, if the garden is to be easily accessible and made good use of, then it needs to be situated close to the indoor space used by the children, so they can move freely from one to the other.

Navigating the garden

Where mobility is an issue, and for those with sensory concerns such as visual impairment, most of the space will need to be level. Distinct paths which are wheelchair-friendly – with smooth surfaces and gentle curves – are ideal.

The minimum recommended width for a path to accommodate one person is about 750 mm or 1,200 mm for two people. A 900 mm width is the minimum for a wheelchair. The turning circle needed for a wheelchair is 1,575 mm for a manual chair, and 2,420 mm for one that is powered.

The surface around beds, raised or otherwise, is an important consideration if they are to be tended by wheelchair users. Bark is not easy to negotiate; a concrete path or decking makes manoeuvring easier.

A continuous path around the garden also enables children to move around the garden easily, but not get lost. Paths can be edged with a different texture, or with a tapping rail, to enable those with visual impairment to navigate more easily. Using loose materials such as gravel on paths is not recommended, as it creates a slip hazard and provides ammunition for those who like to throw. It is also difficult for wheelchairs to negotiate.

Another way to indicate a change of route or level is by including features at different points. This could be a seat, an arbour, a statue or large container, or a specific plant distinctive for some sensory quality such as sound or smell (e.g. bamboo or lavender). Paths, together with these features, help to give the garden a structure – which is particularly important to enable those on the autistic spectrum to make sense of, and feel comfortable in, their environment. This is another reason for using features to create distinctive areas or mark routes, which need to be consistent if they are not to cause confusion and anxiety. The main paths need to be accessible to all, but there can be less formal paths leading off these to other spaces. Dividing the garden up into different areas, and using different levels, means it can provide for varied needs and functions. Should there be the need for steps in the garden, then an adjacent slope, with handrails, will need to be provided for wheelchairs.

Barefoot path

A different idea when considering paths is to create a path intended specifically for walking on barefoot. The idea is to make different surfaces with safe but varied textures, to encourage some children to explore, and to heighten their sensory awareness.

There are many possibilities you could consider and different textures which could be used. Because many of them could be loose, ideally the path should have some sort of edging. Each textured material would need its own edging to contain it: sand, bark, fir cones (*pine* cones are too prickly), larch needles, sawdust, short log stepping 'stones', bark-covered logs (8–12 cm diameter) closely positioned, paving slabs decorated with mosaic or in different shapes and colours, brick paviors, water, mud, wood chips or large cobbles.

For durability, stones and wood blocks could be set in concrete. Areas with loose material such as sawdust could be separated by a smooth hard surface, where they can be naturally rubbed off the feet. The underlying layer in these sections would need to be covered in thick weed-control fabric first, or concreted over. If this is to be an important part of the sensory experience in the garden, then a cover may be needed for sections such as sand and sawdust, when the path is not in use, to protect it from the weather and visiting cats and foxes. Handrails should be fitted if it enables all the children to access the garden. If wheelchair users are also involved, then the materials will have to be particularly well chosen – the children could be helped to feel the different textures with their hands.

Make a significant beginning and end to the route – for example, the path might start with a bench, where shoes and socks could be removed, and end in a rill (or shallow stream) or outside tap, where feet could be washed. Increase the sensory value of the walk with the use of well-chosen plants (see Chapter 5).

Barefoot path

Gardening activity area

The gardening activity area may be a working area with raised beds and a tool shed, perhaps also a polytunnel if space and money allow. Here children can experience planting and harvesting produce, using gross and fine motor skills. This is a place for those with excess energy to do some heavy digging, vigorous sweeping or raking – activities which also help to reduce stress and anxieties in others. These tasks can be very rewarding, and can boost the self-esteem of those who have low self-esteem or none, as they can see the results of their labour.

This is an area where, if appropriate, children could have their own plot or container. Wheelchair users may find raised beds easier, although this involves sitting, twisted, sideways on to the bed unless it is a 'trough' design. To enable wheelchair users to learn harvesting and pruning skills, have a ground-based bed with standard fruit bushes, roses and so on, which can be reached more easily. Another suggestion is to provide a normal table with a grow bag in a tray. The child can then tend their flowers or vegetables, and the whole bag can be placed on the ground for them to water more easily.

If children can choose what to grow and learn to care for in their own plot, they learn decision-making and independence, improving their confidence as a result. Self-esteem is also increased when others enjoy the fruits of their labour and praise their efforts.

The working area would be a good place to have a safe store for gardening tools, preferably accessible for wheelchair users too.

Digging area

Socialising area

Some may want to use the garden to socialise in and perhaps entertain others, so a space could be included with seating and tables, and with room for a barbecue. Here the fruits of their labour can be enjoyed and shared with others.

A learning environment

If the garden is to be used as an alternative learning environment, then seating and tables will be useful for this also. Perhaps a rustic storytelling chair could be included here.

Also consider having a communication board somewhere in the garden, where messages can be conveyed (e.g. 'Please water the sunflowers') or feelings communicated (e.g. 'I enjoyed eating the raspberries'). A communication board is a great asset that will encourage literacy skills and can also stimulate discussion.

Storytelling chair

Communication board

A peaceful haven

Children may benefit from, or seek, a quiet and reflective time on their own. Creating sheltered corners, or arbours with seats, provides children with somewhere to feel safe and calm. Children on the autistic spectrum may particularly appreciate safe havens created in this way when they are 'overloaded' with sensory input.

For others, the more agile and sociable, the arbours give them somewhere to hide and opportunities for play.

Sensory stimulation

Space could be made for vestibular and proprioceptive stimulation for children who enjoy or benefit from additional physical activity other than the garden-related tasks. Use swings and hammocks, ropes, trampolines, equipment or plants to crawl over or under, and a grassy hummock to run up and down on. Ensure there is plenty of space, so that others can keep safe and clear of those on the equipment.

Stimulating other senses can be achieved in many ways in the garden, through the use of plants (see Chapter 5) and in the design and features chosen. Use large pebbles with the sensory stimulus painted on them (e.g. *smooth* leaves, *rough* bark), and place them strategically in the garden. They can act as a prompt for staff unfamiliar with the garden, a prompt for those who can read, and a marker for quizzes and sensory trails around the garden.

Texture can be introduced through different path surfaces, walls, containers and other features, and by using different materials. For example: cobbles, decking, sleepers, slabs, brick or gravel (see also 'Navigating the garden' on page 48). Also consider growing plants vertically, to create a tactile or sweet-smelling wall.

A water feature somewhere in the garden is a great asset. This could be a small pond, attracting wildlife with all its benefits, or a simple fountain. Children can be soothed by the sound of falling water and will enjoy its feel.

☠ Vigorous fountains may stir up airborne pollen and are not recommended for children with allergies.

Introduce additional sounds into the garden with musical instruments, or hang wind chimes where they catch the wind.

Touching and listening to the water

Introduce collections of natural materials, such as cones, shells, twigs and leaves in boxes near to seating areas or tables, for children with limited mobility to explore and investigate.

Wildlife observation

A fascination for wildlife can be nurtured in a garden setting, by ensuring that there is an untidy wild area for wildlife to flourish and hide in, bird feeders, 'bug hotels' (see Chapter 6) and nesting places for birds and insects, with adjacent seats from which children can observe. Include plants which are attractive to birds and insects (see Appendix A). Children who are nervous can gain confidence with insects, as they watch them flying around engrossed in flowers, and not interested in *them*.

Wild area

A real asset in a children's garden is an unstructured area with grass, logs, branches and shrubs. Here they can play freely, or make camps, assault courses or whatever they choose. Include a patch where children can dig for the physical activity, or discover worms, make holes and play with the soil, where no-one has to worry about precious plants being disturbed. For some children this is the closest they may be able to get to 'real' gardening. It can be seen as a valuable precursor to 'productive' activity but also as an undemanding activity that can reduce levels of anxiety.

Research has shown that replacing tarmac with water, woodland and flowers produces a dramatic change in children's social behaviour, their feelings about themselves and their world (Moore and Wong, 1997).

Safe haven

Most importantly, the garden needs to be safe – somewhere where staff know the children cannot come to harm, get lost or wander away. As already described, the garden can include physical and intellectual challenges, but the number of hazards will need to be reduced to the minimum. Make sure that the entrance and exit for the garden are welcoming, encouraging and easy to use. Ideally, do not have too much sensory stimulation at the entrance. Introduce plants and features gradually, so the sensory input is not too great for those who are hypersensitive and may be deterred from entering.

Ease of maintenance

The garden designer needs to be aware that garden maintenance cannot be a top priority either for the children or staff involved. Having fiddly areas that need careful hand-weeding or mowing, or which cannot be maintained easily, means they are likely to be neglected and spoil the overall look of the garden. There needs to be an understanding of how much time can be given to upkeep, and the garden designed accordingly.

Health and safety considerations

The RHS has a very comprehensive outline of all the health and safety considerations which need to be made in a school garden. It is worth looking at its Campaign for School Gardening (www.rhs.org.uk/schoolgardening) to download this information.

Health and safety considerations may be one of the reasons why some people are reluctant to involve children with SEND in gardening. The potential for hazards may seem overwhelming. Here they are broken down into the different aspects to consider.

- **Plants** are the main 'tool' of the horticultural therapist; the sensory value of plants is huge. However, there are also many poisonous plants, and others which can inflict injury if unwittingly handled or ingested (see Appendix A; see Sources of information for a useful book on poisonous plants; and see also the RHS website). Be aware of children's individual allergies (see 'Allergens' below).
- **Plant supports** – canes and sticks are often used to support plants such as tomatoes or sunflowers. Cane toppers should be used, to avoid the hazard of bending down and being poked in the eye. See also Chapter 3 on 'Tools and equipment'.
- **Soil** – chemicals should not be used in a children's garden. Advice on this can be found on the Garden Organic website (see Sources of information). **Organic gardening** is gardening without the use of man-made chemicals either to feed plants or to kill pests and weeds. Consequently it is the safest way to garden to protect

children and wildlife. Inevitably, some children may eat the soil. Sterilised compost may be preferable for such children to handle. Washing hands after handling soil should become part of the gardening routine. Avoid use of animal manures, if children are likely to eat soil and not wash their hands.

- **Wildlife** – insects which sting or bite cannot be avoided, and in fact those such as bees should be encouraged. For children who have the ability to understand, make them aware of the role that such creatures play, and enable them to observe their behaviour from a safe distance. Washing hands after gardening can reduce concerns when children handle worms or other small creatures. Do not garden in an area if it is visited by cats, dogs or foxes.

- **Water and watering devices** – one aspect to consider is that water makes surfaces slippery. Also, trailing hoses create a trip hazard. Water butts should have a child-proof lid. They should not be used as drinking water or for washing hands. Ponds should be covered.

- **Tools** – storing tools correctly is important, as is ensuring that they are in a safe position when put down temporarily. For example, do not leave the teeth of a rake upright so that they can be trodden on. Check regularly that tool parts are secure, are not loose and do not need mending. Sharp tools should be sharp and out of reach of those who cannot use them safely. Children should use an appropriately sized tool.

- **Surfaces** – surfaces intended for wheelchair users need to be suitable. Also, loose gravel or slate, for example, can be difficult for some to walk on. Check that surfaces are not slippery when wet, and check for frost or ice. Algal growth can make surfaces such as decking slippery, especially in winter. This can be improved by covering the area with chicken wire.

- **Weather** – strong winds may cause twigs or limbs to fall from trees. Rain can affect surfaces as already described. Children will need protection from sun, with hats and sunblock, and shaded areas to work in.

Personal protective equipment

- **Footwear** worn by both children and staff should be protective. Ideally wellingtons or work-boots should have steel-capped toes.

- **Gloves** are needed when handling spiky or stinging plants, and if handling manure or fertilisers. Some children may be averse to wearing any, so this may determine which tasks they can participate in.

- **Helmets** should be worn if there is danger of falling timber or if large tools are being wielded.

- **Goggles** should be worn if there is a danger of spray or small pieces going into the eyes.

- **Clothing** – ideally children need to wear tough, weatherproof clothes that they can get dirty. Teenagers particularly may be averse to wearing any sort of warm coat, and may see a visit to a garden to do horticulture as an opportunity to wear their latest trainers. They may need encouragement to wear more suitable clothing. Having a store of waterproofs and hats (charity shops are a good source) can enable gardening to be carried out even in adverse weather.

Allergens

If children using a garden are very allergic to pollen or mould spores, then this should be taken into consideration in garden design, and the activities which they take part in.

Exclude all grasses whose seed heads can cause severe irritation – this includes lawns.

Choose plants which are pollinated by *insects* rather than by wind. This means that many native trees, such as hazel, alder and willow, are best excluded. Choose plants such as Day lily *Hemerocallis*, and *Heucheras*, *Aquilegia*, *Campanula* or roses, all of which are insect-pollinated.

Remove rotting vegetation, including compost heaps, from the accessible area of the garden, as spores will be produced by moulds forming. Keep heaps covered, to discourage the mould spores from fruiting. Do not let allergic children turn and spread compost, or be in the area where this is done, as this will cause them to inhale mould spores.

For gardening with severely allergic children, choose early mornings in spring, or cooler dull days.

CHAPTER 5
Sensory integration in the garden

A garden is the perfect place for enabling sensory integration. People often associate sensory gardens with those with special needs, but in essence all gardens and plants are sensory. However, if children have poor sensory integration, then the choice of plants and features in a garden can provide real benefits (as shown in a study by Hussein, 2010).

Those who have *low* sensory thresholds have difficulties in processing and integrating sensory input. Because the information they receive from their surroundings, which is conveyed to the central nervous system, is reduced, so is their ability to learn, plan and organise behaviour. Some children, notably those on the autistic spectrum, may have heightened sensory thresholds, causing them to 'shut down' if the sensory input is too high for them.

For **hyposensitive** children providing a stimulating environment, and stimulating activities using exaggerated body movement, can improve the ability of their nervous system to integrate the sensory input they receive. Thus their conceptual and motor learning can be improved. All of this can be achieved by passive and active involvement in the garden (see Chapter 1).

For **hypersensitive** children providing a calming space and soothing activities can reduce anxieties and improve concentration and sensory integration.

To ensure that the sensory input for children is at the level where they are not overstimulated or understimulated, make sure that external noises are reduced to a minimum. This may mean, for example, using screens of trees or fencing to cut out the sound of traffic. Use the gentle sound of water to override more intrusive noises from machinery or people.

One of the suggestions in Chapter 4 on garden design includes an area where the vestibular and proprioceptive senses can be stimulated.

The senses of touch, smell, taste and sound can be equally well addressed in the choice of plants, and in the materials used in garden features. See Appendix A for a list of plants that can be used to stimulate the different senses.

If you have a 'barefoot path' (see Chapter 4) included in your garden design, then use this as an opportunity to stimulate *all* the senses by the choice of plants put in alongside. The path is designed to stimulate the sense of touch using feet, but you could plant grasses such as *Stipa tenuissima* to tickle the fingers as you go, smell lavender, see bright marigolds or hear bamboo rustling – and with tasty herbs, you would have a whole sensory experience alongside just one path!

Hearing

The garden will need to be shielded from as much external noise as possible, if the sound of the plants and features included in the design are to benefit sensory integration.

Plants which move and rustle in a breeze, such as bamboo, tall grasses or trees, can be effective. Incorporate wind chimes (maybe ones made by the children), but ensure that these do not become irritating.

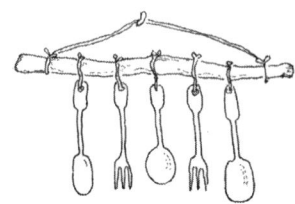
Hang wind chimes where they catch the wind

The seed pods of some plants may produce rattling or gentle sounds when shaken. For example: sweetcorn *Zeamays*; Honesty *Lunaria annua*; dried pods of runner beans, broad beans and peas.

Consider path surfaces. Gravel and slate, for example, create a distinctive sound when walked on; wood or wood chips would be quieter.

Some seed pods rattle when gently shaken

A safe water feature can provide soothing sounds in a garden, and children are always attracted to it. There is a lot of choice these days, with fountains and cascades, and interesting shapes from which water can pour. When choosing, also consider the tactile properties of the fountain, which most children will be eager to touch as the water pours out. A shallow rill could also be used in play activities quite safely.

If wildlife is encouraged into the garden, then birds and flying insects can produce a variety of sounds, which are all the more obvious the quieter the children are. See Appendix A for plants which are good at attracting wildlife.

Smell

Plants with a significant smell can be used as markers, to aid navigation around the garden, particularly for those with a sensory impairment. However, some plants, such as lavender, will only be effective in the summer.

Herbs have the double benefit of producing a significant smell, plus taste, which is why they are a popular choice for a sensory garden. Rosemary, lavender, oregano and thyme all have distinctive smells and tastes, and the added benefit of attracting bees.

Some plants will release their aroma if brushed against, some if they are rubbed between the fingers. Others release their perfume on sunny days. There are several winter-flowering shrubs known for their smell, such as *Lonicera purpusii*.

Perfumed climbing shrubs are effective grown over arbours, creating scented seating corners. Examples are jasmine and honeysuckle. In containers, grow scented plants such as lemon verbena *Aloysia triphylla* – the best lemon scent of all – or *Pelargonium crispum*, the lemon-scented pelargonium. Both of these need protection in the winter. There are other tender pelargoniums, including those with a scent of roses, wood or camphor. In these instances it is the leaves, not the flower, that are perfumed.

Encouraging awareness of smell

Putting scented plants in raised beds or containers enables children in wheelchairs, or with other mobility problems, to enjoy the perfume too.

Touch

All plants have a tactile property, but some are more tactile than others. The leaves, petals, stems and bark can all be considered when choosing plants for this quality. Because they require actual physical contact, they need to be positioned where they can be reached. Raised beds and containers may help, particularly if children are wheelchair dependent.

Exploring the tactile properties of plants

There are leaves which are soft and furry to the touch, such as *Stachys lanata*, *Verbascums*, *Buddleja crispa*, *Lavandula lanata*, *Salvia argentea* and *Pelargonium tomentosum*.

Others are hard and spiky, such as *Mahonia* and Teasel *Dipsacus fullonum*; smooth such as *Cannas* (not **hardy**); waxy, for example *Bergenia* and *Crambe*; or cold, spiky succulents such as *Sempervivum*. The latter can be grown with very little soil on a wall or the edge of a bed. If gently touched with an open hand, they can provide good sensory stimulation, but won't spike the hand. Try growing some in between paving stones, and let the children walk barefoot on good weather days over *Sempervivum* and thymes or use *Chamomile* 'Treneague' (the non-flowering variety of chamomile used for lawns).

Sitting on a chamomile lawn

Petals with good tactile properties include silky Cosmos, Coreopsis and Dahlia, or spiky Echinops.

Papery seed heads include: perennial cornflower *Centaurea montana*; everlasting flowers *Helichrysum monstrosum*; and Honesty *Lunaria annua*.

Tactile tree bark includes that of the cork oak *Quercus suber*; flowering Tibetan cherry *Prunus serrula*; paper birch *Betula papyrifera*; and snake bark maple *Acer capillipes*.

Tactile tree bark

Sight

Think not only about colour and shape in the garden, but also about light and dark. These will be constantly changing depending on the season, the weather and the time of day.

To create a visually stimulating space, therefore, choose vibrant, even clashing, colours with dramatic shapes for a sunny part of the garden. Hang a 'washing line' with coloured cloth, which can blow in the wind and on which shadows of plants can be cast by the sun.

For those who are hypersensitive, create a muted space with plants in gentle tones that blend together. Ensure that there is some shade, and aim to reduce the number of plants that will sway and create a flickering effect in sunny and windy conditions.

Looking at the shape and colour of a sunflower

Taste

A garden can be an ideal setting to introduce children to unfamiliar tastes and textures of edible plants, which they have previously been reluctant to try. Produce that they have grown can be used in soups and smoothies, to make garlic bread or herb scones. The possibilities are endless.

Tasting garden produce

Children can be involved in the whole process of sowing, growing, harvesting and preparing food, and ultimately tasting. The whole range of tastes can be met using garden produce. See Chapter 6 for some ideas. Taste is not just a bout what the tongue detects – smell is also part of the process. Some people have far more taste receptors on their tongue and are hypersensitive to taste. Just as people may see things differently to each other, taste is also subjective.

There are many children with an overpowering need for the sensory stimulation of touching and putting anything and everything in their mouth who, due to poor understanding, are unable to discriminate between which plants are food and which are not. Of course, many plants are poisonous or irritants. If the garden is to be used by any children who are unable to be taught the right and wrong plants to eat, then the garden should include only edible or non-poisonous plants. Those included in the list in Appendix A are either *edible* or *not poisonous* if ingested.

Activities to encourage sensory integration

Collecting

Collect the following on walks around the garden or outside space and use for later sessions indoors if necessary. Also use these items in the suggested manner, as you proceed with the walk:

- rattling — seed heads
- soft — leaves, petals, seed heads (clematis, old man's beard)
- hard and spiky — cones, seed containers (e.g. conkers, acorns), burdock, echinops
- light, gently tickling — feathers, grasses and their seed heads
- soft, dangling — catkins
- brightly coloured — flowers, leaves
- patterned — petals, bark
- sweet smelling, tasty — fruit
- gently rattling — seed pods – dry broad beans, peas or poppies
- smooth, hard — stones
- rough or smooth — textured shells.

Use the collected items with the children for sensory sessions or to stimulate communication and expand vocabulary, and to find out more about the child's likes and dislikes.

Preparing and cooking food

- **Herbs** – collecting, drying, making sachets (see Chapter 6). Taste, make teas, use herbs in cooking. Mix with face cream or make bath bombs.

- **Spices** – are not usually available in the average garden, but are obtained from plants and can legitimately be used to expand a child's experience when part of cooking activities. For example, vegetable soup can be made spicy by the addition of prepared cumin and coriander seeds. Help children to grind these and to enjoy (or not!) the smell of roasting spices. Use these to make spicy popcorn, where you have the added sensory experience of popping corn and a tasty product at the end. All can be linked to gardening.

- **Vegetables** – wash off the dirt (use lukewarm water if the weather is cold), smell, cut up, taste (cooked or uncooked depending on the vegetable). Prepare, cook with, and taste the product.

- **Fruit** – pick, feel, smell, taste. Cut open and touch, taste, cook if necessary. Squeeze the fruit, smell it, rub it onto a white surface, lick the fruit. Find words to describe it, and communicate likes and dislikes. Make a fruit salad. Sow the pips/seeds in pots of compost and watch them grow.

Washing and preparing vegetables to encourage sensory integration

Feeling pumpkin seeds in lukewarm water

Encouraging awareness of trees

- Walk in leaves or rake them up and listen to the sound they make.
- Lie on the ground, look up from a wheelchair, watch the movement and listen to the sound of leaves in the wind.
- Pick a bud and unfurl the new leaf.
- Crunch dried leaves in your hands.
- Smell rotting leaves, and feel the warmth in a pile of them.

- Learn about floating and sinking by putting acorns, conkers and chestnuts in a bowl of water – discover those that float (which are not viable seeds). Bury those that are viable in pots of compost and put them somewhere sheltered outside to chill and then start to grow in spring (cover in chicken wire to prevent squirrels from 'raiding' the pots).
- Listen to the sound of birds in trees.
- Feel the bark, hold a stick, hug a tree.

Appreciating flowers

- Look at flowers for their colour, height, size and shape.
- Feel the petals or the centre (e.g. sunflowers), **dead-head** and shred the petals – what colour do your hands become?
- Smell for their scent, touch for their texture.
- Taste (check they are edible), rattle the seed heads, feel the seed heads and remove the seeds. Use to make shakers.
- Watch flowers moving in the wind.
- Observe wildlife visiting flowers, listen to the hum of insect life.
- Pick and arrange flowers (perhaps with help) to take home.
- Use flowers in cooking.

Observing wildlife

- Listen to the sound of birds singing (recorded or live) or scurrying in the undergrowth.
- Dig into leaf mould or undergrowth and feel the tickle of spiders, the smoothness of earthworms.
- Keep a wormery. Watch the progress of the composting process by the worms week by week.
- Watch dragonflies dart over ponds and frogs gently plopping into water.
- Observe butterflies among the flowers, look for caterpillars.
- Listen to the hum and watch the busyness of bees (from a safe distance if the children are nervous).
- Lift stones and logs, then quickly look to see what is living underneath.

Observing wildlife

Taking a walk in the garden – and giving walks a focus

The following ideas are to give children and supporting staff a focus for their walks around the garden, which can be a good way to start or end the day. Most of them focus on the sensory aspect of plants. A certain amount of preparation may be needed before you can include all of the suggestions, but once this is done, they can be used in future sessions.

It can be worthwhile preparing a simple map showing the paths and general layout of the garden, with features marked on it, such as compost heap, raised bed, fountain. Preparing a map could be an activity in itself, if the children are able. Have photocopies of the maps for some of the following ideas.

For children who are less able, a supporting adult will need to mark things on the map and help keep the child focused on their task.

For each walk you may need a clipboard, some paper and a pen and/or a seed tray.

- Provide children with a piece of fabric (e.g. velvet, towelling, silk, cotton) or paper with different textures, putting one sample at a time in a small seed tray. The idea is to find something in the garden, be it a petal, leaf or piece of bark, with what seems to the child to be a similar texture to the fabric.

- Collect items together at the end of the walk and use for discussion.

- Before the walk, prepare sachets of herbs (see Chapter 6 for a simple method) that are growing in the garden, such as lavender, mint, chamomile, lemon balm, thyme, bay. Do not label the sachets if the children are able to read (you will have to give them a code number instead). Children have a sachet each and have to go around the garden and try to match the smell to a plant. Follow up the activity with discussion and a comparison of likes and dislikes.

- Prepare small seed trays lined with coloured paper, with a different colour in each tray. Children have one tray each or work in pairs. They have to walk around the garden and collect items which are in that colour group. Try to ensure that all seven colours of the rainbow are being collected. Enlist the help of support staff if necessary. When all have finished, there can be discussion of the many and varied hues of the same colour. Arrange the items on an off-white piece of paper to create a rainbow. Make a record of it by photographing your ephemeral piece of art. If it isn't windy, this could be created outdoors.

- Make a seasonal collage. Using a seed tray, collect leaves, petals or twigs during the different seasons and use to create an ephemeral collage to show how the colours in a season change in their predominance. You could then re-create this using coloured paper from gardening magazines. Look at the work of artist Andy Goldsworthy for inspiration (see Sources of information).

- Before the walk, prepare a small seed tray with leaves of plants in the garden. Try to choose distinctive ones, such as oak, sycamore, holly, hollyhock, rosemary. Children have to look for the 'matching' plant and collect another leaf like it. Follow up the activity by identifying the different leaves each child has found, if they are able. There could be discussion about different shapes and colours. If they are able to understand, you could also use this to talk about the role of leaves in plants, what is the common colour in leaves (green **chlorophyll**) and its function.

- A variation is to place a seed pod, flower, piece of a shrub or a piece of fruit into the seed tray and see whether children can find where it comes from in the garden. Provide them with a map print-out, so they can mark their discovery on it. They can then share maps and see whether they can find each other's discoveries.

- Prepare a paper with each child's initial written boldly at the top, fixed to a clipboard. The idea is for the child to move around the garden and discover what they can see, touch, taste or smell that begins with the same initial sound as their name, for example: **S** – sunflower, snowdrops, sun, seeds, squash, swishing, silky.

- An advanced form of this would be to provide each child with their name clearly written across the top of the piece of paper, and they have to observe or collect something to represent each letter. Follow up this activity by asking others to identify what is represented by each letter, and making other suggestions, for example: DANIEL – **d**andelion; **a**nt; **n**est; **i**nsect; **e**arth; **l**eek.

- Back inside, children could use photographs they have taken, or pictures cut out from magazines, to show what they found to represent their name.

- Prepare beforehand by finding very small tins or other containers (charity shops can be a good source of these). Children go round the garden and look for whole items to fit into their tin (e.g. a petal, sunflower seed, stone, leaf). Follow up the activity by looking at each other's finds and comparing discoveries. Count their items. Who fitted the largest number into their container?

- A good end-of-term activity is to provide children with a sheet of numbered photos of different plants or features in the garden. For more able children these can be made harder by just photographing a small part of the feature or plant. This could work well in pairs, with each pair having to identify what the photos are and where in the garden they can be found. Again they could be marked on the map. There could be prizes.

- Focus on sounds in the garden. Prepare by writing a sound boldly on the paper on the clipboard (e.g. HISS, SWISH, SCRUNCH). Children go around the garden listening for their particular sound. These can be marked on the map.

- Talk through their discoveries, and using the map go round the garden using appropriate noises at significant points, i.e. produce a sound map of the garden.

- As an extension of this, use different senses and mark on the map where something was heard, tasted, smelt, touched or seen; essentially creating a sensory map of the garden. Small sticky labels printed with symbols to represent the different senses could be used to mark the significant points on the map. Get other children to trial the maps and see what comments or contributions they make.

- Use a folded fortune teller to guide the children round the garden on a walk. First make a folded fortune teller for each child, or make these in another lesson with the children if they are able to contribute (see Appendix B for instructions). Think about what you want the children to focus on or learn through using these, and label the fortune teller accordingly. These can be tailor-made to suit the age and ability of your group.

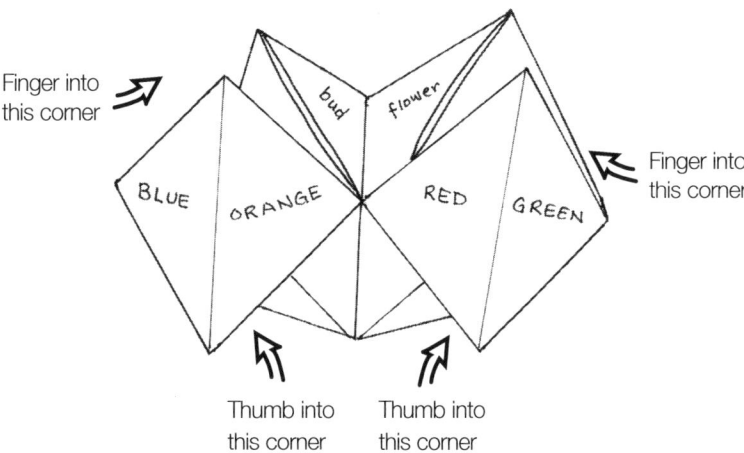

Folded fortune teller

Creating and telling sensory stories

Gardens can be a wonderful source of ideas and props for **sensory stories**, and where better to have sensory storytime than in a garden? Hopefully your garden will have somewhere for a storyteller and children to sit together (see Chapter 4).

Sensory stories are particularly effective for children with PMLD. In the garden there are sufficient resources for all five senses to be stimulated and stories created.

For those unfamiliar with sensory stories, see Sources of information for helpful websites.

CHAPTER 6
Garden-related activities and games

This chapter gives some ideas for practical, garden-related activities and some of their learning outcomes. Try out some of the following ideas – it may also help you to look at the many others described in children's gardening books. Each activity is accompanied by reasons *why* they have valuable learning outcomes.

It is best not to be too ambitious by attempting activities that are far beyond the children's capabilities or understanding. This inevitably means that initially, supporting adults do most of the task. Look for those activities which the children *themselves* can be actively involved in, or respond to, even if it is only a small part of the task. This will boost their self-esteem and feeling of independence. Backward chaining (see Chapter 1) may be appropriate for some of these activities.

This chapter considers the benefits of these garden-related activities and games, and provides instructions for the activities, with useful pictures of the equipment you will need and descriptions of what to do. All activity sheets are provided on the CD-ROM also.

Craft activity: Seed tapes (1)

Make seed tapes to:

- aid seed sowing
- encourage fine motor skills
- involve practical use of maths (counting and measuring)
- provide a sensory activity.

Finished tapes can be packaged attractively and sold as part of a school enterprise project.

This activity works best using small seeds which are not so easy to sow evenly by hand (e.g. carrots, lettuce).

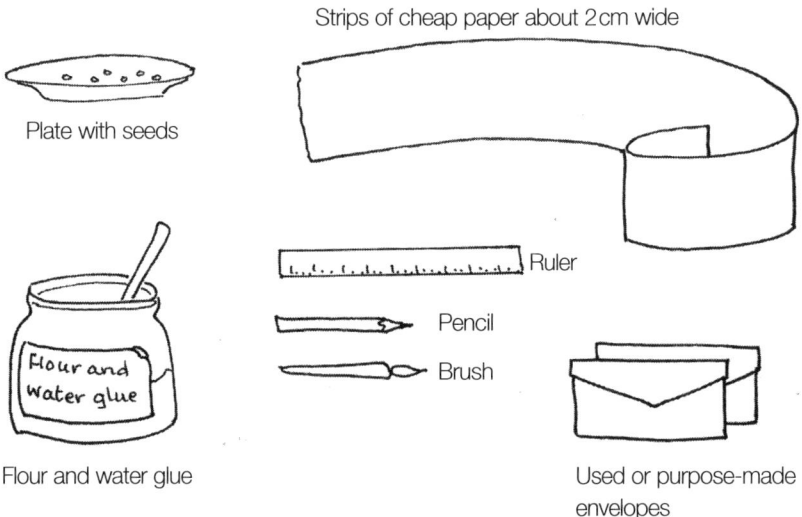

Equipment for making seed tapes

- Cut the cheap-quality paper into 2 cm-wide strips to your required length.
- Fold the strip in half lengthwise.

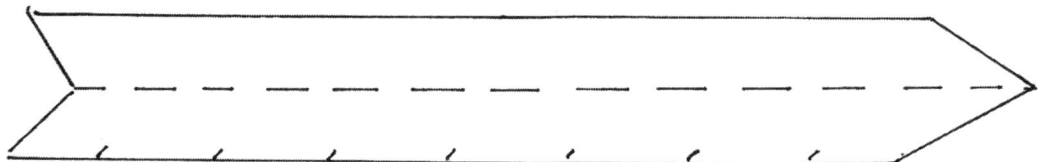

- Using a ruler and pencil, mark along the strip, spacing the marks at the distance required for the type of seed (instructions will be on the back of the original packet).
- Using the brush, place a dab of flour and water glue on each pencil mark.

Craft activity: Seed tapes (2)

- With the seeds on a plate, pick up one seed at a time using a damp brush, and ease onto the dab of glue.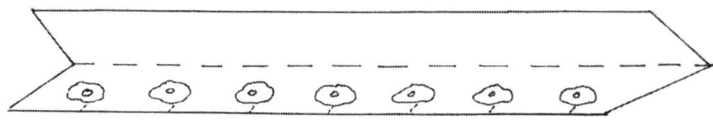

- Fold down the other half of the paper strip to encase the seeds. Leave to dry.

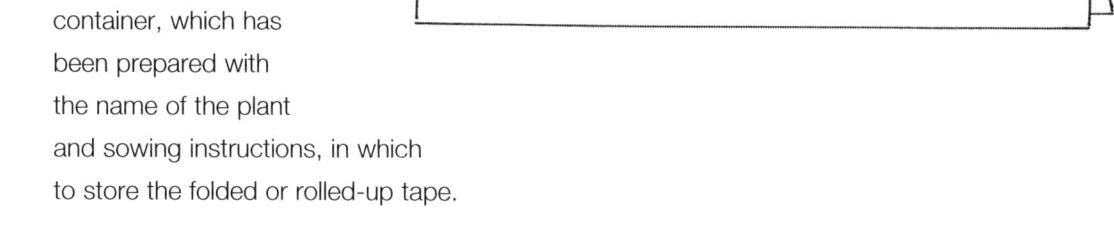

- Use an envelope, or hand-made paper container, which has been prepared with the name of the plant and sowing instructions, in which to store the folded or rolled-up tape.

- Seed tapes can be placed on prepared soil, watered in and covered with soil or compost. Label and water regularly in dry weather.

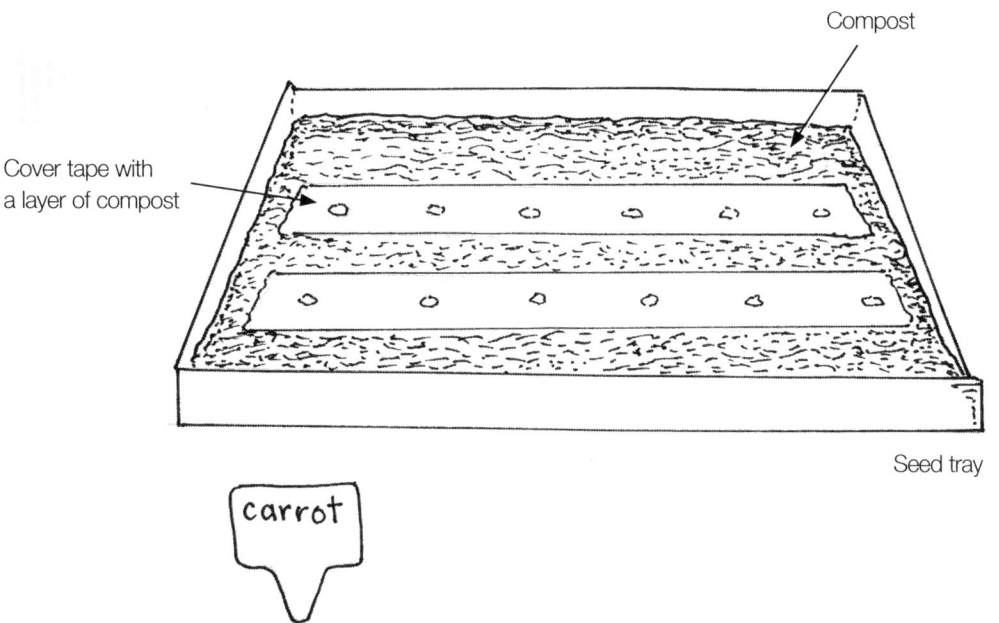

Craft activity: Seed mats

Make seed mats to:

- aid seed sowing
- encourage fine motor skills
- involve practical use of maths (counting and measuring)
- provide a sensory activity.

Seed mats are used to grow plants such as marigolds (*Calendula*) or herbs such as basil or parsley, in pots. You will need the equipment used for seed tapes plus the following additional equipment:

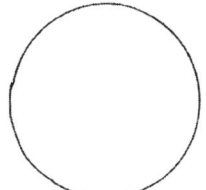 Two circles of cheap paper to fit inside a pot

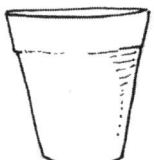 Flower pot

Additional equipment for seed mats

- Cut mats from two layers of the cheap paper, so that they fit neatly into the chosen pot.
- Dab glue evenly onto one piece of paper. Then add seeds to the glue spots and place the other piece of paper on top, so the seeds are sandwiched between the layers. Leave to dry.
- Package as for seed tapes.

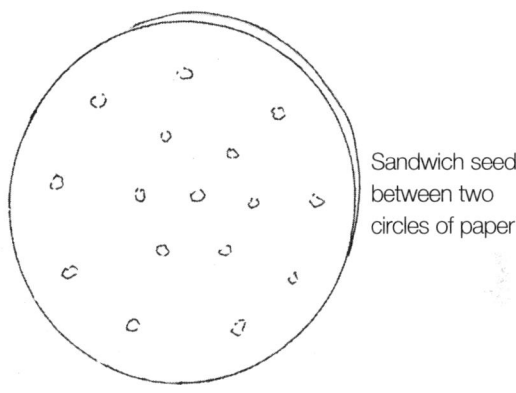 Sandwich seeds between two circles of paper

- Grow by placing on top of compost in a pot, cover with a layer of compost and water in well. Label and water regularly in dry weather.

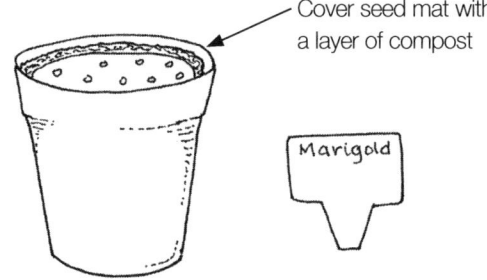 Cover seed mat with a layer of compost

Craft activity: Seed packets

Make seed packets to:

- be the logical conclusion to seed collecting and sorting activities
- use practical maths (counting, weighing and measuring)
- be part of a session using art and design (printing, painting and drawing)
- involve fine motor skills (folding, cutting, sieving, filling, drawing and writing)
- provide a sensory activity (feeling the seeds, sieving through fingers, rattling and shaking seed heads)
- promote literacy skills (writing information and instructions using computer, handwriting, symbols, DYMO printer, etc.).

The finished packets can be sold as part of a school enterprise project.

Garden activity: Bird food

Make food to hang up for the birds to:

- encourage birds to visit the garden, providing more interest and learning for the children
- encourage children to develop an awareness of their surroundings
- provide a good starting point for learning about creatures and their needs
- give an opportunity to learn about *caring* for other living creatures
- provide opportunities for tactile activities and learning some basic science (i.e. the melting of fat, mixing with seeds, pouring into a mould and watching it harden).

Caution: some children respond negatively to the smell of warm fat. (See www.rspb.org.uk for recipes.)

Garden activity: Treasure hunts and trails

Create treasure hunts and trails to:

- reinforce learning
- introduce a sense of competition (if desirable) and adventure
- explore the outside space and encourage observation and movement.

Craft activity: Biodegradable pots (1)

Make biodegradable pots to:

- encourage an awareness of the importance of recycling
- provide an opportunity to learn about which materials can rot – this could lead to scientific investigations
- make planting simpler as they are easier to put in the soil – there is no need to remove the plastic pot first and risk damaging the plant
- broaden children's understanding and experience by using different materials
- provide a problem-solving exercise
- use fine motor skills (cutting, folding, tying, sticking and sewing).

This makes a good problem-solving activity for children who are up to the challenge. It can provide an opportunity for teamwork and a competitive element to be added, if this suits the needs of your children. It makes for a very different lesson than if you were to show them a specific way to make biodegradable pots. The children can amaze you with their ideas and inventiveness.

This project can be undertaken as part of a topic on recycling, use of materials, or life sciences, looking at which materials are able to biodegrade.

On a simple level, bring in examples of materials which can and cannot biodegrade (i.e. can or cannot be put on a compost heap). With the children's help, sort them into the two piles. Examples in the biodegradable pile ('Will rot') could include newspaper, card, wood, cardboard tubes, tissue paper, raffia, string (if cotton), hessian, cotton fabric.

Biodegradable items

Craft activity: Biodegradable pots (2)

The non-biodegradable ('Won't rot') could consist of tin cans, plastic bottles, plastic containers, box cartons, plastic wrappings, tin foil, and so on.

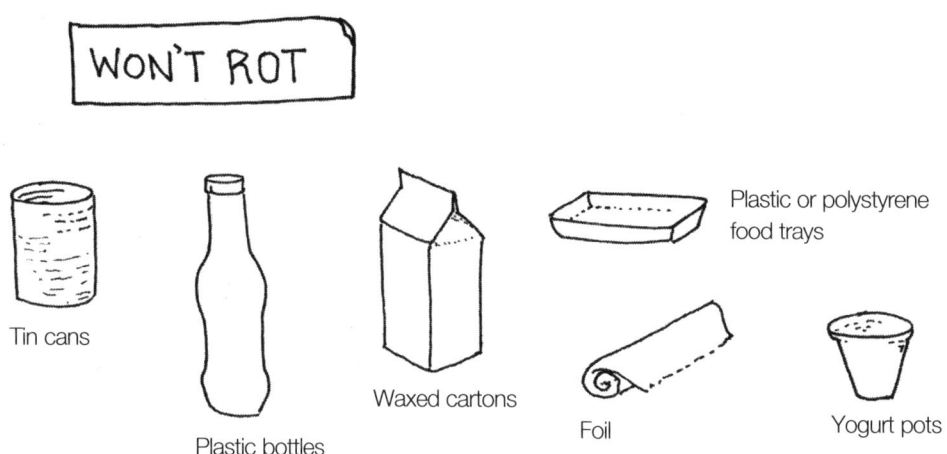

Non-biodegradable items

Then set the children the challenge of making containers into which seeds can be planted, using the materials in the 'Will rot' pile. Lots of useful discussion can ensue with the groups of children about their design. They can fill their pots with compost, sow some seeds or put in a small plug plant, and watch the progress of the plant and its pot.

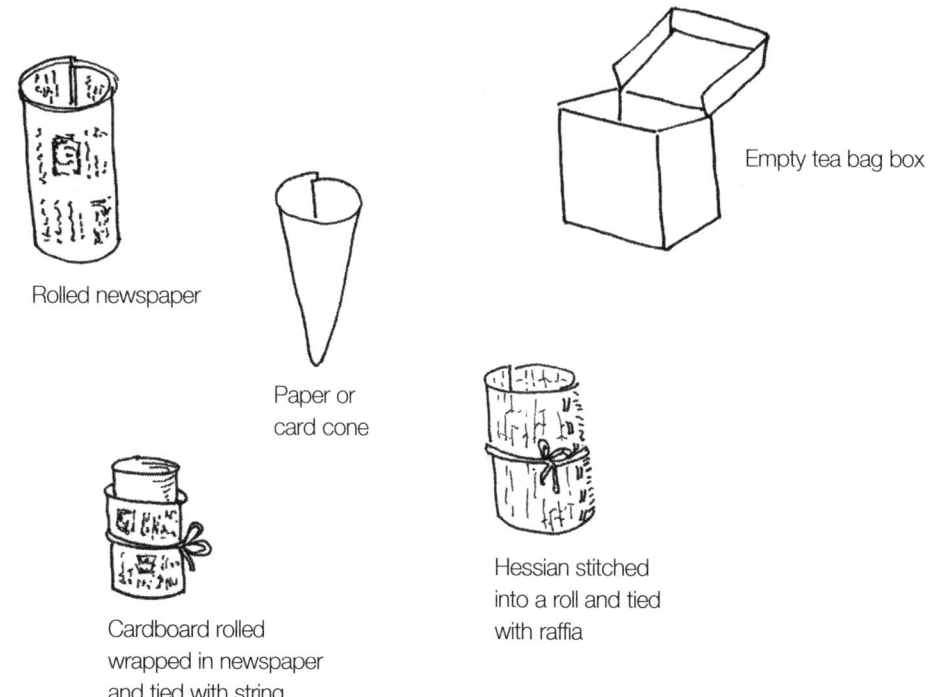

Biodegradable pots

© Becky Pinniger 2015 I *How to garden and grow: gardening as therapy for children with SEND* I LDA I Permission to photocopy

Craft activity: Herb and lavender sachets (1)

Make sachets of herbs or lavender to:

- produce a final product after the sowing, growing and harvesting of herbs
- provide a sensory activity involving picking, shredding and filling of sachets with the lavender/herbs
- use the herb sachets in cooking
- produce finished products which can be part of a school enterprise project or given as gifts.

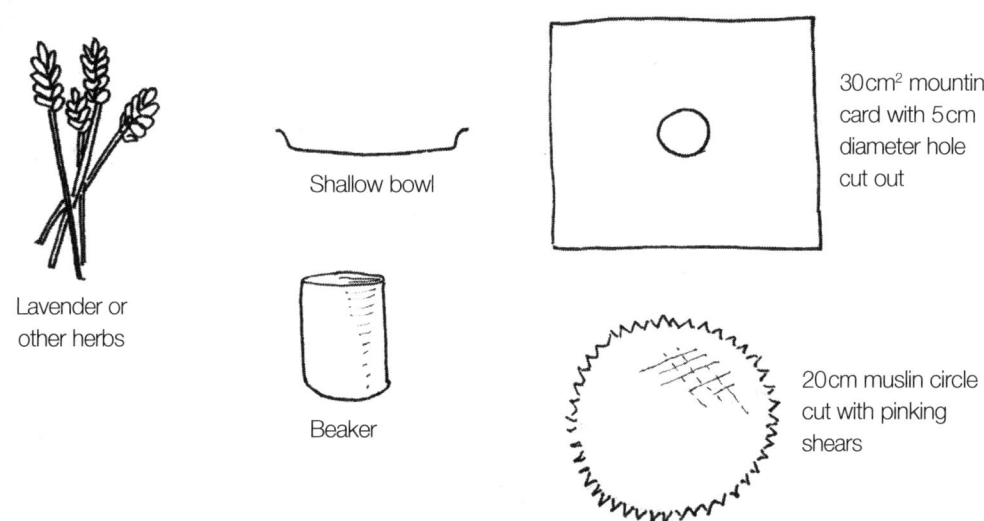

Equipment for making herb or lavender sachets

- Remove lavender heads, or leaves from dried herbs such as thyme, rosemary and marjoram.
- Place mounting card on top of a plastic beaker.
- Lay the muslin circle over the hole in the card.

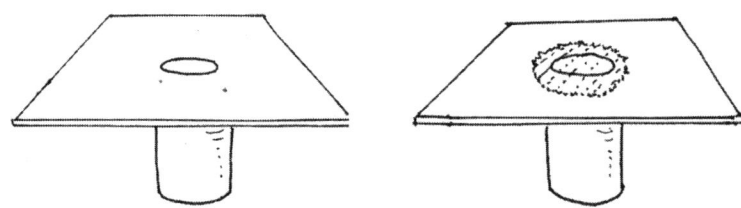

Craft activity: Herb and lavender sachets (2)

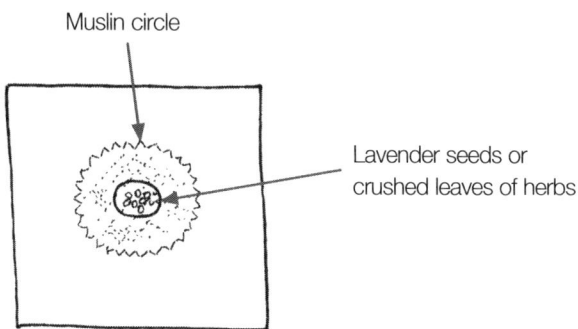

- Pick up a pinch of lavender or cooking herbs and place in the centre of the muslin circle, pushing in slightly so it can hold more. Add more if there is room.

- Using string or ribbon placed under the muslin circle (some children may need help here), bring it round and tie a granny knot so a small bundle or sachet has been made. Remove the plastic beaker.

- Remove the herb sachet from the card by pulling the bag down through the hole and continue to fasten the ribbon or string around the herb sachet into a bow if necessary.

- Sachets can be packaged in jam jars with decorated lids or decorated boxes to give as gifts. Have some lavender sachets hanging in a sensory corner, if desired.

Craft activity: Mobiles and ice mobiles (1)

Make mobiles to:

- create another dimension in the garden, providing sound and movement
- encourage collection and observation in the natural environment, by seeking out suitable materials such as feathers, stones (with holes?), cones, small pieces of wood, twigs, driftwood, seed heads and shells
- involve problem-solving (i.e. how to construct and balance the mobile)
- introduce recycling using manufactured objects to create a mobile (e.g. CDs, beads, cutlery and bottle tops).

Similarly, mobiles made out of ice:

- provide more opportunities for problem-solving
- involve collecting and handling different materials
- introduce more sensory stimulus with texture and temperature of materials and ice
- give an opportunity to discuss the basic science of freezing and melting.

Mobiles consist essentially of a rigid support, such as a twig, driftwood, a metal hanger, or a branch, plus items which can be hung using string, cotton, wire or nylon thread. Items can be collected from the garden, or can be re-used everyday objects, such as cutlery, beads, bottle tops, little bottles. Tying and balancing the strung objects can be tricky, but useful lessons can be learnt and many aspects such as weight, size, sound and balance can be considered.

Ice mobiles are best made when conditions outside are freezing. Their short-term nature can be part of the discussion and learning, but photographs can be taken to preserve their beauty. You can preserve what it looks like but not the feel and smell of the ice sculpture. It could be the starting point for poems or science projects on freezing, and could broaden children's understanding of their world.

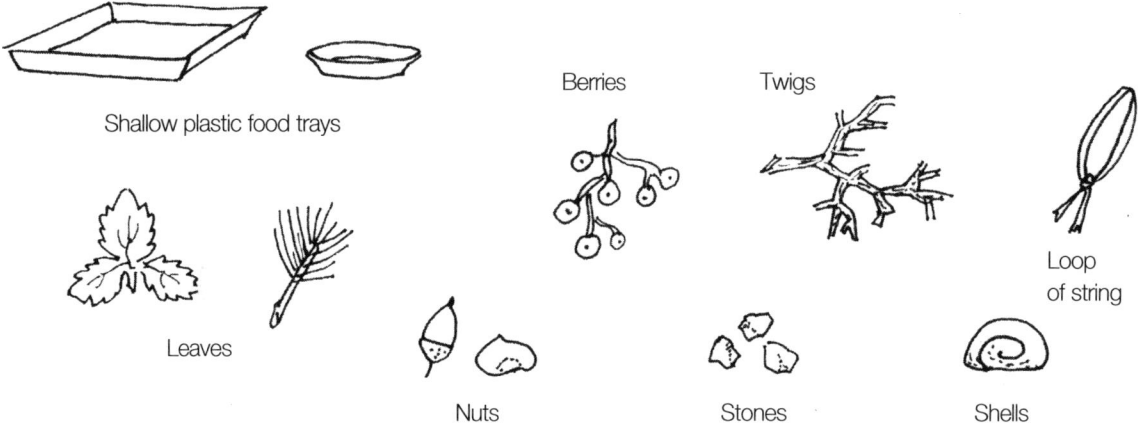

Equipment for making ice mobiles

Craft activity: Mobiles and ice mobiles (2)

- Wrap up warm and go around the garden collecting – small cones, interesting leaves, twigs, seed heads stones, berries, and so on.
- Let children choose some to place in their shallow plastic container.
- Put a loop of string at one end, weighted down with a stone, which can be used to handle the ice mobile.
- Fill the tray almost to the top with water. Glitter could also be added for extra sparkle.
- Leave the trays outside in a sheltered place to freeze.
- Next day investigate, and if temperatures are below freezing, the water will be frozen. Lots of discussion can ensue from this.

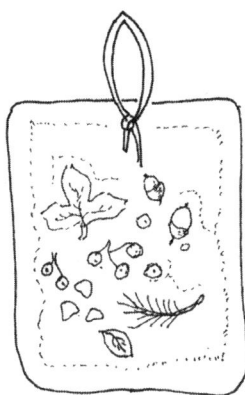

Ice mobile viewed from above

- Ease out the ice shape in which the leaves and berries are embedded. Feel the cold ice, look at and touch the frozen objects. Hang the mobile up by the string on a branch and then take photographs.

Garden activity: Bug hotels

Make bug hotels to:

- provide an opportunity to explore the outside space, looking for suitable materials
- create a chance to handle different materials
- encourage an understanding of the life-cycle and habitat requirements of mini-beasts
- encourage curiosity and observation
- involve problem-solving
- provide an opportunity for teamwork.

Creating a bug hotel consists of making small niches and spaces for a variety of creatures to shelter and lay their eggs. In a woodland area or uncared for green space there are numerous places for creatures to inhabit, such as log piles, rotting tree stumps, under piles of rotting vegetation, and in cracks or crevices in walls or fences. Neat gardens may not provide wildlife with as many shelters, so bug hotels can be built to encourage a healthy population of mini-beasts to thrive in a garden environment.

There are no precise instructions for making a bug hotel. This is where you can let the children's creativity and building skills come to the fore.

Explore the garden for sticks, leaves, pieces of stone, brick or slate, old clay flowerpots, hollow stems of cow parsley or similar, hazelnuts and fir cones. Small pieces of sawn-up log, cut-up garden canes, old clay roof tiles, old bricks with holes and pieces of broken flowerpots are also useful.

Items suitable for bug hotels

If you want to build a large structure, then old pallets can provide an effective framework in which to place this assortment of materials. Holes can be drilled into the ends of sawn-up logs, to provide solitary bees with a place to lay their eggs. Fill old tins or flowerpots with cones, stones or bundles of twigs. Bundles of hollow sawn-up canes can be secured with plastic-coated garden wire. Use an old crate, wooden box or drawer in which to stack these items, or construct a larger frame for them from old pallets. Alternatively place them in sheltered corners of the garden.

Build the bug hotel in a shady part of the garden, and have a seat nearby where children can sit quietly and observe the comings and goings of bees, woodlice and other creatures.

Building and repairing a bug hotel is a good outdoor activity in the depths of winter, when jobs in the garden are few and far between.

Board and dice games

Games such as Bingo and Pairs can be used:

- as a fun way to reinforce learning
- as part of the summative assessment process
- as a good wet-weather activity.

Make the games plant- and garden-related. Gardening magazines and catalogues are a useful source of pictures. The Woodland Trust (see Sources of information) is an equally good source when looking for images and ideas for games that can be photocopied and used in a variety of ways.

Photocopiable images

Equipment for Pairs

- Photocopy pictures (e.g. from the Woodland Trust), of leaves or common weeds, whatever you can find. Cut out, stick on card and laminate.
- Turn pictures face down, two of each picture, mixing them up well.
- This is a memory game, but can be developed further by asking the children a question when they make a pair, for example: 'What type of tree is this leaf from?'; 'Is the tree **evergreen** or **deciduous**?'; 'What is the name of this flower?'; 'What time of year would you sow the seeds of this flower?'; 'Is this a root vegetable?'.

See also Appendix B for other ideas for games.

Miniature gardens

Make miniature gardens to:

- give a purpose and focus when exploring the outside space
- provide an opportunity for individual creativity and choice
- encourage use of fine motor skills (i.e. cutting, placing and constructing)
- encourage recognition of shape and size
- provide an opportunity for problem-solving activities (e.g. how to create a pond, a path, a swing or an arbour in miniature).

Craft activity: Natural paints

Make natural paints to:

- broaden understanding and knowledge of the use of plants
- provide an opportunity to study basic science – the properties of different plant parts, and where some dyes come from
- provide a sensory activity involving harvesting, crushing and spreading of berries, leaves and petals
- encourage creativity and literacy, by using the paints to write or paint with (using natural materials for tools, such as pieces of stick)
- provide an opportunity to talk and learn about colour.

Make the paints from gathered berries and/or petals and leaves. The berries can be squashed and applied with a brush or stick. The petals can be directly rubbed onto paper.

Craft activity: Plant labels

Make plant labels (other than for the very good reason of registering the plant's name) to:

- encourage use of fine motor skills and practical use of writing/literacy skills
- create an opportunity to explore different ways of making labels (i.e. problem-solving)
- involve different ways of writing labels, using technology, pens/pencils, letters and symbols
- enable a greater understanding about the nature and use of different materials.

Craft activity: Seed bombs

Make seed bombs to:

- provide a sensory, stimulating task using different materials and textures
- offer an opportunity to learn about the science of seeds, their dispersal and their growing requirements
- make the children aware of the properties of different materials
- enable children to enjoy throwing the bombs (into an empty field or plot), which can be physically satisfying and challenging for some.

Seed bombs are a fun, and environmentally sound, method of distributing seeds in an uncultivated, unstructured part of a garden. It can be an enjoyable and easy way to spread seeds of native wildflowers.

Seeds can be gathered from wild grasses and hedgerow flowers, such as cow parsley, for a 'harmless' mix to distribute along the edge of a field or alongside a school hedge, for example. The protective coating of clay deters mice and gives the seeds a greater chance to germinate successfully.

Equipment for seed bombs

Work on a tray or similar, and preferably use hands!

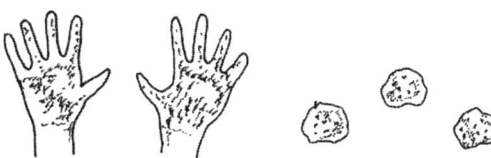

Seed bombs: use your hands!

- Break up hard lumps of school craft clay (not the self-hardening kind) into a powder using an old rolling pin or similar.
- Break lumps of compost and mix with powdered clay.
- Stir in wild flower mix or other seeds.
- Add water to make a mixture that will stick together – very sticky but satisfying.
- Make the mixture into balls (roughly the size of a table-tennis ball) and leave to dry for about a week.
- Once dry, the balls can be easily handled. Take the children to the area where the seeds can be sown. If they have the strength to throw hard, stand well back and turn the session into a competition, if that is what they enjoy: 'Who can throw the furthest?' or 'Who can hit the target?', and so on.

Craft activity: Cooking

Cooking is the final stage of – and the logical conclusion to – many gardening tasks involving fruit, vegetables, edible flowers and herbs. Like gardening, cooking is an opportunity to learn science – for example, the difference between a fruit and a vegetable, and the names of the different parts of plants. Children can observe change brought about by heat and physical processes and the nature of different materials.

- It encourages use of fine motor skills, which are needed in chopping, peeling and grating, plus gross motor skills in mixing, beating and grinding.
- Cooking is an activity that uses all the senses.
- It is an opportunity to learn about the origins of food, covering aspects of both geography and history.

Products can be used to share with others, which may encourage social skills and be the starting point for a school enterprise project.

- It can involve practical use of literacy and numeracy skills, such as pricing ingredients, estimating and calculating the cost of the product, labelling, marketing and selling.
- In early summer, pick and wash mixed lettuce leaves, violas, marigold petals and herbs. Shake off the water and create a thing of beauty in a pretty bowl to take home for tea.
- Pick and wash fruit to stir and make into jam to eat with scones or toast.
- Pick and wash a mixture of herbs. Smell their leaves, and your fingers, then chop the leaves finely. (A safer way to chop herbs is to put the washed herbs in a small tumbler, and chop with scissors.) Stir into a scone mix, made by rubbing butter into flour, adding cheese and a little egg to make a dough mixture, then cook in the oven and enjoy the smells once more. See how the mixture has become firm and the texture crumbly, flecked with the green from your herbs. Enjoy as part of lunch, perhaps after the group has been tying up bunches of herbs to sell as bouquet-garni.
- Try grinding basil, browning pine nuts, and adding crushed garlic and grated parmesan for a stimulating sensory experience. Think of the smells, sounds, textures and tastes which are part of this activity. Finally, eat the finished pesto stirred into warm pasta or spread on a toasted baguette.
- In autumn, chop up and roast the inevitable pumpkins, along with onion and garlic. Save the seeds for more recipes or craft activities later. Roast, grind, smell and stir in spices with the pumpkin, onion and garlic mix. Blend and eat the soup on a cold day after a chilly morning in the garden raking leaves, or after planting garlic for next year's soup.
- Wash, chop and prepare freshly harvested vegetables and fruit, together with spices and herbs, and turn them into jars of chutney to take home or sell as part of a mini-enterprise.

The possibilities and potential of cooking as part of gardening with children with SEND are endless, and you can soon learn to recognise the value of each step and ingredient involved. Try to choose recipes that will involve the children and arouse their senses. You cannot always predict what they will eat. Children often eat 'hidden' vegetables, or new foods they profess to hate, once they have been involved in their growing or preparation.

CHAPTER 7
Assessing the value of gardening

Assessment, and keeping a record of what the children have been doing and achieving, is very much part of a school's remit. A record is a useful tool to monitor a child's progress, whether it is in their behaviour, understanding, development or wellbeing. It can also be part of formative assessment of the child and used to inform planning and target-setting.

Recording hard outcomes

Hard outcomes, which include levels in numeracy and literacy, are relatively straightforward to assess and record. Key stages or P scales can be used as a framework to measure these in most children. As described in previous chapters, gardening activities can be linked with the national curriculum. Skills development, considered in steps or stages, can also be recorded specifically, and gardening skills can be part of this assessment.

Task analysis

Using **task analysis**, gardening tasks can be broken down into clear steps, which involve cognitive or physical processes. See the example 'Lattice system for task analysis: harvesting lavender' diagram opposite. This diagram could be used to record skills development, adding dates on which the steps were achieved.

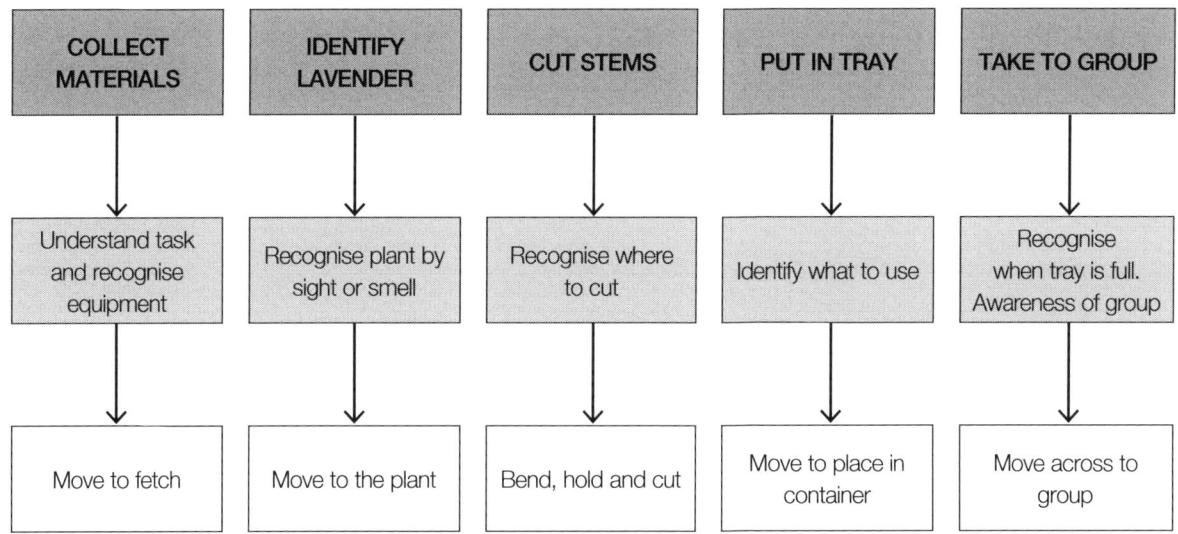

Lattice system for task analysis: harvesting lavender

For qualifications such as ASDAN, there are assessments specifically set out to record achievement for each unit.

SMART targets

When recorded information is gathered, it can be used to inform planning and to determine which tasks are particularly beneficial to meet the child's needs. This information can be used when setting new **SMART targets**. These targets are defined as:

- Specific
- Measurable
- Achievable
- Relevant
- Time-bound.

SMART targets are useful when planning which learning skills to teach a child.

SCRUFFY targets

It is worth noting that children with severe learning difficulties (SLD) or profound and multiple learning disabilities (PMLD), and whose development may not be linear, may benefit from having **SCRUFFY targets** (Lacey, 2010). By definition these are:

- Student-led
- Creative
- Relevant
- Unspecified
- Fun
- For Youngsters.

SCRUFFY targets are useful when preparing to build up a child's understanding prior to more specific skills-based learning.

Recording soft outcomes

Some way of recording the achievements of soft outcomes is equally important, and can be used as a measure of the benefit that children may have gained through gardening. Soft outcomes may include:

- social skills
- co-operation
- concentration
- independence
- self-confidence
- self-esteem
- teamwork
- empathy
- contentment.

Ways of recording soft outcomes are less obvious. Children enjoy looking back on what they have done in the garden. A record can be a useful resource to encourage conversation or other interaction, which in itself may provide more information on a child's development and understanding. It may also enable a level of self-assessment by a child, using their preferred method of communication.

A scoring system

A scoring system can be useful for a child who may find it hard to describe how well the day has gone, for example:

- 5 = the day went really well
- 4 = I had a good day
- 3 = I enjoyed some of the day
- 2 = I found some of the day difficult
- 1 = I did not enjoy the day.

It is often revealing to discuss with the child the reasons for the score they give each session. It may be one 'small' occurrence that makes a child score 1, while most of the session may have gone well. It can also demonstrate some 'improvement' (or not!) in their levels of enjoyment.

In end-of-lesson 'social time' when the session is discussed, it can also be informative to receive similar feedback from the staff, together with their reasoning. For example, a teaching assistant may say: 'I give today 4, because my student worked really hard and I enjoyed seeing their progress'.

Record sheets

As part of self-assessment, more able young people could make a record of:

- what they think they did well during the session
- how they could do even better
- what they need to learn to do next.

Record sheets could be discussed with staff and also used as part of the formative assessment process.

Providing a record enables parents and carers to have a better understanding of their child's school day, and the importance of gardening in improving their lives. The child can share what they have done with their parents and other carers, who can then help to reinforce their learning with similar activities at home. Grandparents can play an important role in this – it is often they who have the time and skills to share a garden with their grandchildren.

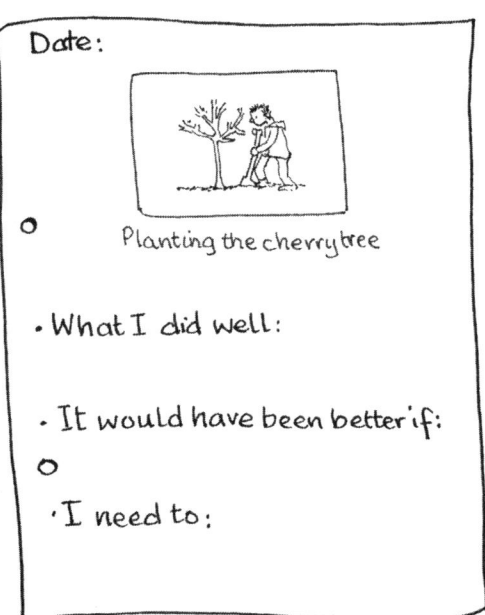

Example of a record sheet

Recording activities

Recording activities can be done in several ways.

Photographs

If at all possible, it may be worth designating a member of staff to take regular photographs during part of a gardening session. Photographs can be of children demonstrating particular skills or carrying out specific tasks, or can show their mood as they relax or sit quietly. The pictures can be used for the record and for stimulating discussion and reinforcement of tasks with children. Children can also take and use photographs for this.

A record written by staff

For some assessment purposes, for example when doing qualifications, specific witness statements by other members of staff or volunteers can be used to record children's achievements. At other times, staff may want to record small steps as they occur, using sticky notes, which can be discussed and used as evidence later.

Using sticky notes to record progress

Comments made by the children during or after a session can similarly be recorded. Children with poor concentration can be timed doing certain tasks and their levels of concentration monitored regularly.

Children's 'written' records

A child's 'written' record may be in the form of a diary or comments about the session's activities, using handwriting, a word processor, Makaton or dictated to staff. It may also take the form of a letter, for example to the head of the school or an organisation supporting the school, informing them of what they are doing and learning.

Children could keep a personal gardening diary in a scrapbook, notebook, folder with plastic sleeves, hand-made book, or even on the computer (e.g. as a blog). This could include photos, which may be of the child in the garden working on tasks, or of their plot. The child may be able to take their own photographs, or do their own illustrations, or use cuttings from gardening magazines, seed packets, etc. Writing can be done in person, dictated, using a word processor, or voice recognition device, using symbols or prepared stickers that the child chooses.

Sharing a gardening diary with a grandparent

Drawings

Drawings can be made by the children, showing what they have done and how it made them feel. They could be used to produce posters that demonstrate a child's knowledge and understanding, and this can be used for formative assessment purposes.

Video/audio recording

End-of-session discussions could be recorded as evidence. Activities or specific tasks carried out in the garden by children could be recorded. Children could use this technology to present information to an audience and, if they have the skills, to make a PowerPoint presentation to other pupils, staff or parents.

Likewise, children can operate the recording devices or hold 'interviews', which will say a lot about their technical as well as their communication skills.

Reward systems

Behaviour charts and other systems already in place in a school setting can be extended to gardening sessions and used to assess a child's behaviour, not only in the sessions, but also whether the activity seems to be having an impact on their behaviour generally.

Sadly, missing a gardening session may be used as a form of 'punishment' for children presenting with challenging behaviour, particularly if they look forward to the session. This seems self-defeating.

Hand-outs

Hand-outs with multiple-choice questions, or gaps for children's own answers, can be used to demonstrate a child's knowledge and understanding of tasks in the garden, which they may or may not be able to complete independently.

Quizzes and board games

Quizzes written specifically to assess a child's knowledge of activities and what is growing in the garden can be a useful tool in assessing how much they have absorbed.

Equally useful as a summative assessment tool are self-made board games with questions aimed at the level of knowledge the children are expected to acquire.

End products

Children may be involved in garden-related craft activities or other activities which result in an end product, for example a hanging basket, a bowl of bulbs, a bird house or a bug hotel. These end products can be photographed and used to assess how much the children were able to do independently, whether they recalled the whole process or needed support. All of these can help to assess a child's progress.

At the heart of all assessments should be the needs of the child and meeting those needs. Recording, whether by children or staff, enables the benefits of gardening to be seen and valued by both.

End products can be photographed for assessment purposes

Garden and (watch your children) grow

If you work with children in a garden setting, whatever their needs or ability, it doesn't take long before you realise the benefits they gain. You can visibly see their anxieties lessen as they become engrossed. You observe them becoming more self-confident, with greater feelings of self-worth as they achieve and communicate with others. For children with a severe disability, you can see them relaxing and at the same time enjoying the stimulation of the sensory environment created in a garden.

Making gardens and gardening accessible for all children opens up a whole new world of possibilities and can be enormously rewarding for everyone. Enable your children to garden and grow – in every sense of the word.

Gardening can be very rewarding

CHAPTER 8
A year-round programme of activities and tasks in the garden

The tasks outlined in this chapter are relevant to all gardeners, whether or not they have any special needs. Some children with disabilities will not be able to do all these activities, but by adapting the approach, environment and resources (as outlined in Chapter 1), they could be possible.

Be guided by the weather rather than the actual month of the year.

Material from this chapter is also available on the CD-ROM.

January

Outdoor gardening	Indoor gardening	Crafts and activities
Harvest vegetables.	Wash vegetables in lukewarm water.	Make soup. Use uncooked vegetables to print with and for still-life drawing, painting and collage.
Plant garlic.	Plan what to grow in the coming season. Plant garlic cloves into 9 cm pots to transplant later.	Sort out seed packets. Use découpage to decorate a seed container using seed catalogues. Make a folder of recipes using garlic; try some out, e.g. garlic bread and pasta sauce.
Sow broad beans and sweet peas.	Understand seed packets. Sow broad beans, sweet peas, onions, leeks and lettuce in modules for transplanting later. Make long pots with newspaper rolls suitable for peas and beans.	Make a seed packet for saved seeds.
Plant up pots for spring colour.	Plant up pots for spring colour.	Decorate pots prior to planting.
Spread compost onto beds.	Take cuttings of houseplants and arrange the cuttings in pots of pebbles.	Make music shakers or mobiles using dried saved seeds.
Learn about the different parts of plants. Collect examples from the garden.	Learn about parts of plants. Play the 'Growing Paper Plants' game (see Appendix B).	Draw plants or parts of plants, using chalks, charcoal or paint.
Rake and sweep leaves.	Birdwatching and recording in a book the birds seen.	Make bird feeders, bird houses, bird tables.
Do a winter hunt around the garden.	Garden games – word search, Bingo and Pairs (see Chapter 6).	Use objects found on a garden hunt to create collage. If cold enough, make ice sculptures to hang outside (see Chapter 6).
Force rhubarb.	Bring in branches of spring-flowering shrubs to force blooms to open early; use in arrangements.	Make bird tables, nesting boxes, homes for bumblebees and ladybirds. Make a booklet of rhubarb recipes.

© Becky Pinniger 2015 I *How to garden and grow: gardening as therapy for children with SEND* I LDA I Permission to photocopy

February

Outdoor gardening	Indoor gardening	Crafts and activities
Prune gooseberry bushes and shrub roses.	Chit early potatoes.	Make a miniature garden in a tray (see Chapter 6), using succulents.
Lift and divide overgrown perennials.	Sow perennial seed such as *Penstemon* and *Rudbekia*.	Make pancakes and find out about the plants the ingredients come from.
Divide snowdrops and winter aconites and replant.	Divide snowdrops and winter aconites. Talk about parts of plants.	Draw flowering bulbs or take photographs of them for a display.
Put fleece or black plastic on beds to warm soil.	Sow tomatoes and peppers.	Prepare a recipe using tomatoes and peppers, such as salsa, and sow some of the pips. Make a link between the plant and the seed.
Empty the compost bin or turn compost.	Grow plants from pips. Grow the top of a pineapple. Try planting a piece of ginger root, or a stem of lemon grass.	Make tropical fruit salad.
Clean and sort out shed and tools.	Clean hand tools and oil them.	Decorate and mark out a plank for measuring distances when seed sowing.
Wash pots.	Wash pots.	Sort pots by size and shape. Use them to make a 'pot figure'.
Harvest vegetables.	Wash vegetables in lukewarm water. Visit a market vegetable stall or a good display in a supermarket to see the variety of vegetables.	Make soup. Buy something new to try, research recipes. Vegetable printing, drawing. Investigate where different fruit and vegetables come from.
Cut back (to the ground) canes of autumn-fruiting raspberries.	Plant cuttings of autumn raspberries into medium-sized pots. Sow seeds indoors of tomatoes, peppers and salad crops.	Make a collage or a mosaic from dried collected seeds.
Use willow or hazel whips to plant and create a fence, wigwam, tunnel or den.	Make plant supports from willow or hazel coppicing for containers.	Make miniature woven structures indoors. Make a 'bird's nest'.
Do a winter quiz walk around the garden.	Prick out seedlings of seeds sown in January.	Prepare labels using different ideas, ready for future use.

March

Outdoor gardening	Indoor gardening	Crafts and activities
Plant hardy perennials, such as Michaelmas daisies and *Rudbekia*. Plant evergreen hedging.	Clumps of perennials can be divided up in the greenhouse or polytunnel to plant outdoors later. In the meantime, plant the divided pieces into pots. When the soil has warmed up, these can be taken out of the pots and planted in the ground outside.	Make labels for perennials.
Mulch borders using compost, leaf mould or wood chips (the latter only around mature plants). Spread wood chips over depleted paths.	Pot up rooted cuttings of houseplants taken in January.	Decorate pots to hold houseplants. Make labels with name of plant and care instructions. Hold a plant sale to raise funds.
Prune winter-flowering shrubs and coloured stems of dogwoods.	Make hardwood cuttings from dogwood prunings.	Use dogwood prunings and other natural materials to weave and create 'nests'.
Start sowing seed outside if the ground is warm enough* (e.g. chard, salad, beetroot, peas, parsnips and spring onions).	Sow indoor carrots, chillies, peppers, cucumbers and salad.	Use carrots or beetroot in a recipe such as soup or salad. Roast vegetables to relate to the seeds sown.
Maintain planted spring containers, by weeding and feeding with 'tomato food'.	Plant up a pot for Mother's Day, e.g. with violas, pansies, primroses, ivy or Bellis (daisy).	Decorate a container or pot for Mother's Day prior to planting.
Dead-head bulbs that have finished flowering and feed the bulbs.	Make seed tapes (see Chapter 6).	Use seeds packaged by children and organise a 'seed swap' as a fund-raiser with parents and staff.
Weed beds and containers.	Identify which weeds to put on the compost heap and how to deal with perennial weeds.	What can rot and what cannot? Make biodegradable containers from recycled materials (see Chapter 6).

* *You will know when the soil is warm enough, because small annual weeds will start to appear.*

April

Outdoor gardening	Indoor gardening	Crafts and activities
Sow herbs: parsley, marjoram, thyme and chives. Sow leaf beet, spinach, beetroot, carrots, lettuce, peas and mangetout peas.	Sow herbs: parsley, marjoram, thyme, basil or chives in pots for the windowsill.	Decorate pots prior to planting if to be used for gifts/sales. Make decorative and informative labels.
Take cuttings from mature, woody herbs, such as thyme, sage, rosemary, lavender hyssop and bay.	Make cuttings from the herbs, put into small pots with well-drained compost. Plant summer-flowering bulbs such as *Gladioli* or lilies.	Use herbs in a recipe such as herb scones.
Sow hardy annuals outside in the position they are to flower, such as marigolds (*Calendula*), *Godetia* and *Alyssum*.	Sow large seeds in pots, e.g. sunflowers, ornamental gourds and nasturtiums.	Make plant labels.
Plant early potatoes.	Plant early potatoes in containers indoors for an earlier crop.	Cook with potatoes to link to the planting activity (e.g. potato pancakes or stuffed baked potatoes).
Weed beds and containers.	Identify which weeds to put on the compost heap. Find out how to deal with perennial weeds.	Using objects, create an informative poster with themes such as: 'Making homes for wildlife', 'Five weeds to look for in the garden', 'Plants we can eat'. Make biodegradable containers from recycled materials.
Lift and divide crocus. Divide primulas.	Divide clumps of bulbs indoors, prior to replanting outside. Divide primulas. Plant summer-flowering bulbs in pots (e.g. *Gladioli* or lilies).	Make labels for summer-flowering bulbs.
Trim and prune evergreen hedges (not if the weather is frosty, as new leaves could blacken).	Prick out and pot on seedlings that have grown (see Chapter 2).	Crafts for Easter: plant a basket; make a nest to hold sweet eggs, using colourful or flexible twigs such as hazel.
Plant out beetroot and carrots, sown earlier indoors in modules, after hardening off. Sow directly into the soil.	Sow more carrots and beetroot in modules for successional sowing.	Make carrot cake or carrot soup to relate to the seeds sown.
Prepare a trench for growing beans and put in plant supports.	Sow French and runner beans in modules.	Make bird scarers. Find out how to deter slugs and snails organically; make and place traps.

May

Outdoor gardening	Indoor gardening	Crafts and activities
Put in hardy annual bedding plants, e.g. snapdragon, marigold (*Calendula*), poached egg plant, *Godetia*, candytuft.	Prick out and pot on.	Make a collage of a summer garden, using old seed packets and seed catalogues.
Lift spring bulbs out of pots and tidy spring borders. Keep the bulbs somewhere dark and cool, ready to replant in the autumn.	Start to plant up hanging baskets or other containers. Keep indoors until all danger of frost is over.	Hold a fund-raising plant swap with parents and staff (e.g. tomatoes, peppers, lettuce and herbs from cuttings).
Harvest vegetables.	Wash vegetables, or bag up to sell or take home.	Make a salad on a plate, or sandwiches with home-grown salad, perhaps for a picnic.
Weed beds and containers.	Identify which weeds to put on the compost heap. Find out how to deal with perennial weeds. Photograph some weeds to aid identification.	Make biodegradable containers from recycled materials. Use photographs to create a poster to aid weed identification.
Water beds (if dry weather) and containers.	Water indoor newly sown plants and containers.	Make a map of the garden and include points of interest. These can be individual, with favourite places marked.
Sow seeds and French and runner beans in early May.	Sow seeds, French and runner beans, basil in pots or modules to bring on indoors.	Make seed containers and labels from recycled materials.
Plant *Gladioli* and lilies outside.	Sow assorted seeds to use as 'micro-greens' in salads/sandwiches.	Make pesto from basil and garlic.
Prick out and pot on plug plants (see Chapter 2). Harden off summer bedding.	Prick out and pot on plug plants.	Paint stones with the different senses indicated (with an eye, an ear, and so on) and place in the garden at suitable points of interest.
Pick flowers for taking home as arrangements or posies (throughout the flowering season).	Make up posies and arrangements.	Press flowers and use later for cards and pictures.

© Becky Pinniger 2015 | *How to garden and grow: gardening as therapy for children with SEND* | LDA | Permission to photocopy

June

Outdoor gardening	Indoor gardening	Crafts and activities
Stake tall-growing perennials. Plant perennials or shrubs.	Take softwood and semi-ripe cuttings of shrubs (see Chapter 2).	Paint, sketch or photograph individual plants and garden scenes. Relate to a specific artist, such as Monet or Georgia O'Keeffe.
Trim evergreen hedges.	Take cuttings of shrubs (e.g. hyssop, box or shrubby honeysuckle).	Create miniature gardens in trays (see Chapter 6).
Collect seed of spring-flowering biennials (e.g. foxglove, sweet william).	Sow collected seed in trays or modules.	Make seed packets for collected seeds.
Harvest summer salads and fruit.	Harvest summer salads grown under cover. Wash salad leaves.	Make salad with leaves and flowers.
Plant out salad grown as plug plants.	Sow more salad in modules for planting out later.	Make strawberry compote and use to fill a flan, or make strawberry pavlova.
Plant out bedding plants in beds or containers.	Plant up containers to put outside.	Press flowers for craft; use petals for pot-pourri. Use marigold *Calendula* to make soothing face cream or to add to small cakes for colour.
Pick and dry herbs.	As a sensory activity, shred herbs to be used for herb sachets. Use herbs to make cuttings (see Chapter 2).	Make sachets of herbs as gifts or to sell, and for sensory activities.
Weed plants in beds and containers.	Weed beds of crops grown indoors.	Make tomato salsa with tomatoes, peppers and cucumber to eat with crispbread.
Water all containers – and beds, if weather is dry.	Water all indoor-grown plants and containers.	Plan a summer picnic/barbecue.

July

Outdoor gardening	Indoor gardening	Crafts and activities
Prune spring-flowering clematis and honeysuckle.	Sow biennial seed, e.g. wallflowers, foxglove, sweet rocket.	Take photos of the garden and display them as a poster or in a book.
Harvest vegetables and fruit.	Harvest vegetables and fruit and wash them.	Prepare vegetables or fruit as salads, smoothies, soups or jams and chutneys. Have a barbeque or a picnic prepared with as many home-grown ingredients as you can.
Do pond watching and pond dipping.	Look at mini-beasts through magnifiers. Draw an illustrated food chain of the garden.	Draw creatures seen in the garden. Make clay models of them. Do quizzes and play games linked with wildlife.
Collect seed heads and seeds.	Shred and dry seed heads.	Make and decorate packets for seeds. Make seed tapes with collected seeds for the new gardening year, or to sell as a mini-enterprise.
Weed beds and containers.	Weed indoors – if you have a polytunnel or greenhouse. Harvest and tie in tomato plants.	Harvest and dry tomato seeds and create seed packets for sale.
Pick and dead-head flowers.	Arrange flowers.	Make a miniature garden.
Harvest lavender for drying.	Shred the dry lavender heads prior to making into sachets.	Make lavender sachets. Use lavender seeds in recipes such as biscuits.
Sow salad for autumn and winter harvest.	Sow salad for autumn and winter harvest.	On a cool day, make jam with harvested fruit.
Harvest onions, shallots and garlic.	Plait onions, garlic and shallots. Once dried, hang in a cool, dry place to store.	Use onions in recipes such as soup, quiche and garlic bread.

August/September

Outdoor gardening	Indoor gardening	Crafts and activities
Plant out biennials raised from seed. Plant out bedding for spring, such as wallflowers, forget-me-nots, primulas, violas and pansies.	Grow autumn crocus* in water.	Bake using seeds such as sunflower, pumpkin or linseed. Make muesli or bread rolls using seeds.
Plant spring bulbs outside: daffodils,* hyacinths* or snowdrops.*	Plant early-flowering hyacinths* indoors.	Decorate plant pots prior to planting with bulbs.
Tidy borders, by cutting down dead heads and stems, and weeding.	Tidy indoor growing areas.	Sort out seed packets. Use old ones to create a collage of a garden.
Collect and sow seed from the garden.	Package collected seed, or make seed tapes/mats (see Chapter 6).	Design seed packets.
Save and **stratify** seeds of trees.	Test seeds for viability – will they float or sink in the bucket of water? (If they sink, they are viable.)	Use conkers and acorns to create models or figures.
Sow spinach, rainbow chard, turnips, beetroot and Japanese onions.	Sow parsley and winter salad indoors.	Cook some of the vegetables that you used for the seed-sowing activity, as soup or in a risotto.
Secure strawberry runners in soil, so they can take root. Runners resemble thin roots coming from the main plant above ground, which have the beginnings of a new plant growing on the end.	Pot up strawberry runners, once rooted.	Make scones to eat with strawberry jam (made in June/July).
Empty hanging baskets and compost the contents.	Empty hanging baskets. Plant up baskets for winter show, using small shrubs, ivy, heather, pansies or violas.	Start a pictorial or recorded diary of the garden. For a book, use children's drawings or pictures cut out of gardening magazines.

These plants are poisonous or irritants

October

Outdoor gardening	Indoor gardening	Crafts and activities
Take hardwood cuttings.	Take hardwood cuttings.	Hold a garden quiz or play a garden game (see Chapter 6 and Appendix B).
Continue planting bulbs. Plant up a container for winter interest.	Continue planting bulbs. Plant up a container for winter interest.	Create or decorate a container for winter bulbs.
Plant spring-flowering perennials sown in early summer, such as foxgloves, wallflowers or sweet william.	Sow hardy annuals from seed collected in late summer, such as Californian poppy (*Eschscholzia*), marigold (*Calendula*) and love-in-a-mist (*Nigella*).	Use pressed flower heads to make notebooks, bookmarks and pictures.
Collect and sow seed from berry-bearing shrubs.	Stratify tree seeds, then put outside to overwinter.	Sort seeds into 'sets'. Store in jars to use for craft.
Harvest vegetables.	Make a quiz to identify the roots, leaves, stem and flower of different vegetables. Wash vegetables in lukewarm water.	Make a vegetarian pasta meal.
Cut roses back. Cut down buddleja by half, to reduce risk of wind damage during winter.	Sow sweet peas into long pots or root trainers.	What can rot and what cannot? Make biodegradable containers from recycled materials.
Harvest a pumpkin and compost the remains of the plant.	'Investigate' a pumpkin (see Chapter 10).	Use dried seeds to fill a plastic bottle and make a music shaker. Make a necklace or collage from dried seeds or pips.

© Becky Pinniger 2015 | *How to garden and grow: gardening as therapy for children with SEND* | LDA | Permission to photocopy

November

Outdoor gardening	Indoor gardening	Crafts and activities
Move seedlings into the protection of cold frame or greenhouse.	Prepare bird food using seed and melted fat.	Make a bird feeding station and feeders. String peanuts together to hang up for birds.
Take hardwood cuttings from dogwoods, willow, flowering currant, blackcurrant, rose, spirea and viburnum.	Pot up cuttings.	Play a garden-related game (see Chapter 6 and Appendix B).
Rake and sweep leaves. Put them in a leaf mould area or specially made bin of chicken wire. Look for skeleton leaves.	Feel the different textures and shapes. See who can identify them using touch only. Investigate the importance of leaves for plants.	Press leaves and use for art activities. Make leaf impressions in rolled-out clay to create plates.
Turn compost. Investigate wildlife by digging in a full compost heap.	Make a display of creatures found in the compost. Draw up a food chain. Sieve some compost and investigate what hasn't rotted well.	Make creatures to create a display using card/modelling materials. Make a collage from found objects.
Cut down perennials, such as Michaelmas daisies, hardy geraniums, *Rudbekia* and *Helenium*.	Sow sweet peas in deep pots or root trainers.	Make biodegradable pots (see Chapter 6).
Harvest vegetables and green tomatoes.	Sow broad beans, hardy peas and mangetout in modules.	Make pumpkin soup or pie. Roast pumpkin seeds. Make chutney or marmalade with green tomatoes.
Plant tulips in ground.	Plant tulips in containers.	Decorate pots ready for planting bulbs. Make decorative labels.
Plant onion sets and garlic.	Plant onion sets and garlic in modules.	Cook recipes using onions and garlic.

December

Outdoor gardening	Indoor gardening	Crafts and activities
Collect cones, twigs and greenery for decorations.	Make Christmas decorations, table centres with candles or wreaths.	Use fir cones to create different decorations.
Sow sweet peas and broad beans.	Sow sweet peas and broad beans in modules to plant out later.	Make biodegradable pots (see Chapter 6).
Plant garlic.	Plant garlic in modules to plant out later.	Make garlic bread or other recipes with garlic to relate to planting.
Go for a brisk walk, especially after a hard frost or snow. Look for footprints, patterns and icicles.	Create an indoor garden using succulents and indoor plants.	Create a collage of cold colours and features in a winter garden, using cut-up old Christmas cards.
Take hardwood cuttings from dogwoods, willow, flowering currant, blackcurrant, rose, spirea and viburnum.	Pot up cuttings.	Use twigs and other items from the garden to create a textured, tactile board. Make a poster to help identify the different twigs.
Install a bird-feeding station and hang prepared food. Listen and watch for birds.	Make a bird seed cake for the birds.	Colour and cut out birds for tree decorations or to hang on decorated twigs for indoors.

A year-round programme for young people with profound and multiple learning disabilities

This programme is designed to stimulate the senses of young people who are functioning at a very basic level and with profound disabilities.

Activities for adults supporting the young people are included, which can be done alongside the young person or with them, whichever is appropriate.

Autumn (September–November)

Theme	Senses used	Activity for young person	Activity for supporting adult
Vegetables 1 (pumpkins, marrows, cucumbers)	smell, sight, taste, hearing, touch	Look at and feel pumpkins, marrows, cucumbers (the fruit and the leaves). Tap and listen. Cut open and do the same. Remove seeds, feel in a bowl of warm water (see Chapter 10).	Use vegetables for making soups and stews. Remove, wash and dry seeds to use with collage and craft activities and spring sowing.
Vegetables 2 (root vegetables)	smell, sight, taste, hearing, touch	Pull out or dig up root vegetables. Compare shapes and sizes. Feel them and then wash them in warm water. Smell them raw and taste them cooked.	Prepare vegetables for tasting. Sow broad beans, garlic cloves.
Leaves	smell, sight, hearing, touch	Go outside, watch and feel the leaves falling. (See also the suggestions for winter.)	Collect and press different-shaped and different-coloured leaves. Use for craft and mobiles, stick on the window, make rubbings.
Seeds	smell, sight, taste, hearing, touch	Shake and listen to seeds in seed pods. Shake seeds out, or shred dead heads to release seeds.	Make a dry seed arrangement. Store seeds to sow in spring. Design and make seed packets (this can be a gluing activity using magazine pictures). Taste and cook edible seeds such as sunflower and pumpkin.

Winter (December–February)

Theme	Senses used	Activity for young person	Activity for supporting adult
Wet and dry leaves		Feel individual leaves, rummaging in piles. Look at the wildlife living inside piles of leaves. Smell them, listen to the sound of dry leaves being moved.	Sweep, rake up piles of leaves. Collect them in sacks or heaps.
Bark on different trees		Feel the textures. Smell and listen to the sound when they are tapped with sticks, hands, stones.	Build a collage using natural materials to create the texture of bark. Make bark rubbings.
Seeds, conkers, acorns, pumpkin, sunflower, etc.		Eat edible seeds. Make shakers using tins and plastic pots containing different-sized seeds, listen to the different sounds, shake along with recorded music. Make bird cake using seeds and melted fat. Feel pumpkin seeds in a bowl of warm water.	Make musical instruments. Bake seeds in bread/biscuits. Pot up tree seeds and leave outside to grow your own trees. Sow cress, grow sprouting seeds. Use seeds to make textured collage. Sow broad beans, sweet peas.
Seasonable vegetables		Wash dirty vegetables in warmish water using hands. Smell and taste uncooked vegetables whole or grated. Sort by shape or colour.	Use vegetables to make soup for all. Create a 'vegetable tops' garden, by growing tops on damp paper in a saucer, and watch them sprout again. Grate vegetables and make winter salad.
Wind		Make coloured flags out of fabric to fly outside on a windy day. Go outside and feel the effect, watch and listen to the trees.	Make 'windmills' or kites to show the effect of wind. Make wind chimes using shells or bamboo.
Fruit		Help remove seeds from fruit. Fill pots ready to sow seeds. Eat fruit salad or smoothies.	Prepare familiar and more exotic fruit for salad or smoothies. Tap large fruit such as squash or pumpkin and listen to the sound they make.
Evergreens		Feel the different shapes and textures of evergreens. Smell the strong scent and look at the different colours.	Use foliage to make a seasonal decoration for the table or the door.
Garlic		Remove the papery outside of the garlic, take cloves apart. Crush the cloves and smell them.	Make garlic butter to eat with bread. Plant garlic cloves in pots.
Bulbs		Help fill pots prior to planting bulbs. Watch each week as they grow.	Plant bulbs in pots for Christmas presents or spring flowers. **NB: daffodils are poisonous, and hyacinths are sprayed with chemicals.** ☠

Theme	Senses used	Activity for young person	Activity for supporting adult
Ice and natural objects	touch, sight, smell, hearing, taste	Feel the frozen shapes (ready prepared) and how they melt in the hands. Feel the twigs as they emerge from the thawed block. Look in the garden for icicles and footprints. Taste frozen fruit juice.	Put twigs and berries into shallow dishes of water to freeze outside (or in the freezer). Freeze freshly squeezed fruit juice.
Compost	touch, sight, hearing, taste	Feel and touch compost at different stages of decomposition. Tear newspaper and card to add to the heap. Add peelings and waste to the heap.	Turn the heap. Shovel into containers to add to beds.
Pots	touch, sight, hearing	Using a bowl of warm soapy water, wash old flowerpots using hands or a brush, then rinse in clean water. Stack pots, sort by size and shape.	Support young person with activity. This is a good sorting exercise.

Spring (March–May)

Theme	Senses used	Activity for young person	Activity for supporting adult
Leaves, buds	touch, sight, taste	Feel catkins and buds. Unfurl new leaves from buds. Feel sticky buds.	Go for a walk to look for buds and new leaves, catkins. Pick an arrangement of tight buds and watch them open indoors.
Seeds	touch, sight, smell, hearing, taste	Find seeds inside fruit such as tomatoes, peppers. Fill pots with compost and sow seeds that children have found. Sow seasonal flowers and vegetables from packets. Use large seeds, such as beans, sunflowers, marigolds.	Sow smaller seeds into pots filled by children, ready for pots and beds in the garden. Sow pots of herbs for the windowsill and to add to cooking.
Wildlife	touch, sight, hearing, taste	Watch and listen to birds, bees and butterflies. Feed birds (see under 'Winter' in table above). Feel in leaf litter, turning over compost to look for wildlife.	Go round the garden, looking under stones or logs. Encourage stillness to observe wildlife. Make a stick collection to add to a bug hotel.
Walking in the garden (on a warm day when the grass has been cut)	touch, sight, hearing, taste	Smell and feel newly cut grass. Look at new plants and seedlings emerging. Feel the soil.	Be still, watch and listen.
Salad vegetables and edible herbs	touch, sight, smell, taste	Feel and smell the leaves, radishes and other plants. Wash and taste the vegetables.	Make a colourful salad to eat.

Theme	Senses used	Activity for young person	Activity for supporting adult
Flowers	(smell) (sight) (touch)	Match colours, choose some to pick. Smell and touch flowers.	Plant up tubs or hanging baskets, using seeds sown or plug plants.
Potatoes	(smell) (sight) (touch)	Plant potatoes into containers or raised beds. Feel the soil. Cover the leaves as they emerge.	Support a young person with the activity.
Herbs	(smell) (sight) (taste) (hearing) (touch)	Pick herbs, or choose ones to pick. Remove lower leaves. Fill pots with compost and add pieces of herb for cuttings. Help water the plants. Taste the cooking with herbs, and help with baking where possible.	Cut herbs, label pots. Pot on when ready. Use herbs in cooking, soups, herb butter, bread and scones.

Summer (June–August)

Theme	Senses used	Activity for young person	Activity for supporting adult
Flowers	(smell) (sight) (touch)	Look at, pick and smell flowers in the garden. Remove petals, squeeze and rub them over card. Match colours.	Pick flowers and use to make an arrangement or flower garland. Press flowers.
Grasses, bamboo	(smell) (sight) (hearing) (touch)	Listen to them in the wind. Feel seed heads and leaves.	Sow seeds from grasses. Do weaving with grasses. Use bamboo stems to create sound.
Summer fruit	(smell) (sight) (taste) (touch)	Taste, smell, squash and touch summer fruit.	Make smoothies or fruit salad. Cook rhubarb and make crumble.
Aromatic herbs	(smell) (sight) (taste) (hearing) (touch)	Smell, touch, crush, taste. Help to use in cooking and tasting. Pick, dry and crush herbs for use in cooking. Help with making lavender bags.	Make lavender bags, bouquet-garni bags, 'tussie mussies' (posies). Small jars of herbs for presents. Use basil to make pesto sauce and eat with crackers or bread. Harvest lavender for drying.
Seeds	(smell) (sight) (taste) (hearing) (touch)	As for winter and spring. Sow seeds of autumn-flowering plants. Collect seeds from the garden, e.g. shred heads of marigolds to release seed.	Help with sowing and collecting seed. Sow sweet rocket, sweet william and wallflowers.
Salad vegetables (tomatoes, peas, beans)	(smell) (sight) (taste) (hearing) (touch)	Pick, squeeze, smell, taste and feel.	Make tomato ketchup. Cook with beans.

Theme	Senses used	Activity for young person	Activity for supporting adult
Walk in the garden in the sun	(touch) (sight) (taste) (hearing) (smell)	Feel hot stones, contrast with cool water. Watch flying creatures. Taste fruits, vegetables. Sit still and enjoy. Smell the leaves of herbs used for cuttings. Smell the fruit and vegetables in the garden.	Do the same alongside the child or young person.
Cuttings	(touch) (sight) (smell)	Remove leaves, fill pots and insert cutting to increase stock of plants.	Make cuttings of herbs, houseplants, succulents, shrubs.

CHAPTER 9
A seasonal programme with learning outcomes

It can be helpful to consider all the possible learning outcomes of tasks before deciding on which activity is suitable for an individual child. Here are some examples of hard and soft outcomes resulting from each task. The more you do, the more you will become aware of the value of different activities. This chapter is also available on the CD-ROM.

Hard outcomes are considered to be those which are measurable in some way; *soft* outcomes are more tenuous, so are not as easily measurable.

Mastering the practical tasks, whether independently or as part of a team, will inevitably raise a young person's chances of employment, and thus acceptance within society.

Autumn (September–November)

Activity	Hard and soft outcomes
Plant early-flowering hyacinths in pots.	• Fine motor skills: handling soil, filling container, planting bulb. • Encourage literacy: writing label and care instructions. • An activity that involves following a sequence. • Provide an opportunity to nurture. • Encourage social skills and thought for others (by using pot as a gift). • Work as a team (each child has one part of the whole task). • Develop independence.
Collect seed from garden plants or vegetables.	• Fine motor skills: collecting seed, putting it into a container. • Gross motor skills: moving around garden. • Improve memory of the route round the garden. • Encourage an awareness of surroundings. • Ability to follow a sequence. • Ability to follow instructions. • Awareness of cycle of life, parts of plants. • Ability to work as a team. • Develop independence.
Plant spring bulbs outside.	• Fine and gross motor skills. • Digging holes: physical activity involving gross motor skills. • Follow a sequence. • Follow instructions. • Work as a team. • Give an understanding of passage of time and the seasons. • Ability to nurture.

Activity	Hard and soft outcomes
Plant container for winter interest.	- Fine motor skills. - Follow a sequence. - Follow instructions. - Understand plants and their needs. - Learn to nurture. - Social skills: preparing a gift. - Encourage confidence – an immediate result for a morning's work. - Work as a team. - Make choices. - Develop independence.
Harvest vegetables.	- Physical activity: gross motor skills. - Understand about parts of plants, edible and inedible. - Use tools as instructed. - Understand food and where it comes from, nutritional value. - How to use vegetables, prepare something tasty. - Sensory quality of vegetables when washing them.
Make soup.	- Fine motor skills. - Follow instructions. - Develop life skills. - Care and use of tools. - Understand edible parts of plants, and what part of the plant the vegetables are (e.g. root, leaf or stem). - Importance of good hygiene. - Basic understanding of how vegetables can be made into something nutritious and satisfying. - Sensory qualities of process. - Teamwork. - Develop independence.
Rake and sweep leaves.	- Physical activity involving gross motor skills. - Care and use of tools. - Follow a sequence. - Follow instructions. - Develop understanding and awareness of the seasons. - Understand life-cycles, rotting process, composting. - Improve self-esteem – the task makes a clear difference immediately. - Teamwork. - Develop independence.
Prune buddleja.	- Physical activity. - Follow instructions. - Follow a sequence. - Improve self-esteem, provide job satisfaction, make a clear difference in a short time.

Winter (December–February)

Activity	Hard and soft outcomes
Sow sweet peas and broad beans.	❀ Follow a sequence. ❀ Fine motor skills. ❀ Understand and be made aware of the cycle of life. ❀ Teamwork. ❀ Develop independence.
Plant garlic.	❀ Follow a sequence. ❀ Fine motor skills. ❀ Teamwork. ❀ Sensory qualities of activity. ❀ Develop independence.
Make bird feeders or bird houses.	❀ Follow a sequence. ❀ Physical activity. ❀ Care and use of tools. ❀ Awareness of the needs of wildlife. ❀ Care for others, nurturing. ❀ Job satisfaction and self-esteem.
Prune gooseberry bushes.	❀ Follow a sequence. ❀ Fine motor skills. ❀ Awareness of need for care with spiky bushes. ❀ Understand plants and their needs.
Make tropical fruit salad, sow pips.	❀ Follow a sequence. ❀ Fine motor skills. ❀ Care and use of tools. ❀ Understand about parts of plants and the role they play in the cycle of life. ❀ Teamwork. ❀ Introduction to new tastes and smells.
Wash pots.	❀ Follow a sequence. ❀ Understand about plants and diseases. ❀ Sensory enjoyment of warm soapy water. ❀ Job satisfaction and self-esteem. ❀ Teamwork.
Make garden from succulents on a tray.	❀ Fine motor skills. ❀ Understand the needs of different plants. ❀ Awareness of different kinds of plants. ❀ Sensory quality of different components of garden – soils, gravel and soft plants. ❀ Improve self-esteem by creating something living and attractive.
Birdwatching and recording.	❀ Improve focus and concentration. ❀ Literacy skills in recording what birds have been seen. ❀ Encourage observational skills. ❀ Enjoyment of surroundings. ❀ Greater understanding of plant and animal life around us and its varied needs. ❀ Sensory aspects of activity, sight and sound.

Spring (March–May)

Activity	Hard and soft outcomes
Lift and divide perennials.	❀ Follow a sequence. ❀ Physical activity: gross motor skills – can lead to an improvement in mood. ❀ Understand plants and how they grow. ❀ Learn about increasing stock of plants at no extra cost. ❀ Teamwork.
Mulch borders.	❀ Follow a sequence. ❀ Physical activity: gross motor skills – can lead to an improvement in mood. ❀ Understand how to maintain a garden and suppress weeds. ❀ Care of plants and garden. ❀ Teamwork.
Sow seeds indoors – vegetables, herbs and flowers.	❀ Fine motor skills. ❀ Follow a sequence. ❀ Understand more about plant life-cycles and the seasons. ❀ Teamwork. ❀ Sensory aspects of task. ❀ Develop independence.
Plant up early potatoes.	❀ Physical activity: gross motor skills – can lead to an improvement in mood. ❀ Understand food and where it comes from. ❀ Link cooking activity for sensory enjoyment.
Weeding.	❀ Fine or gross motor skills. ❀ Physical activity – can lead to an improvement in mood. ❀ Job satisfaction. ❀ Teamwork. ❀ Develop independence.
Take herb cuttings.	❀ Fine motor skills. ❀ Follow a sequence. ❀ Understand plants, how they grow and their value to people. ❀ Teamwork. ❀ Sensory experience of handling herbs. ❀ Develop independence.
Trim and prune evergreen hedges.	❀ Physical activity and gross motor skills. ❀ Care and use of tools. ❀ Job satisfaction and self-esteem. ❀ Understand the need for continuing care and nurturing of plants. ❀ Teamwork.
Start to plant up hanging baskets.	❀ Fine motor skills. ❀ Follow a sequence. ❀ Make choices. ❀ Understand plants and their needs, nurturing. ❀ Social skills: preparing a gift. ❀ Encouraging confidence: an immediate result for a morning's work. ❀ Teamwork. ❀ Develop independence.

© Becky Pinniger 2015 | *How to garden and grow: gardening as therapy for children with SEND* | LDA | Permission to photocopy

Summer (June–August)

Activity	Hard and soft outcomes
Harvest summer salad.	❀ Fine motor skills. ❀ Follow a sequence. ❀ Teamwork. ❀ Social skills: sharing and selling produce.
Plant perennials and shrubs.	❀ Physical activity, gross motor skills. ❀ Follow a sequence. ❀ Plan. ❀ Make choices. ❀ Understand the needs of plants, nurturing.
Pick and dry herbs including lavender.	❀ Fine motor skills. ❀ Sensory enjoyment from task. ❀ Follow a sequence. ❀ Teamwork. ❀ Develop independence.
Weeding.	❀ Fine or gross motor skills ❀ Correct use of tools ❀ Improve self-esteem: the task produces a satisfying result. ❀ Teamwork. ❀ Follow a sequence. ❀ Recognition of which plants to remove.
Watering.	❀ Physical activity, gross motor skills. ❀ Understand needs of plants. ❀ Sensory aspects of feeling, watching and listening to water. ❀ Follow a sequence. ❀ Develop independence.
Pick strawberries, raspberries and currants; make smoothies.	❀ Fine motor skills. ❀ Follow a sequence. ❀ Sensory aspect of task: touch, smell, taste. ❀ Teamwork. ❀ Social skills: sharing produce.
Sow biennial seeds – foxglove, wallflowers.	❀ Fine motor skills. ❀ Follow a sequence. ❀ Understand about plant life-cycles and the seasons. ❀ Teamwork. ❀ Develop independence. ❀ Sensory aspects of task.
Mow lawn, trim hedges.	❀ Follow a sequence. ❀ Know how to use tools safely. ❀ Physical activity, gross motor skills. ❀ Teamwork. ❀ Improve self-esteem: the task has a clear, effective outcome. ❀ Develop independence.

CHAPTER 10
Developing a scheme of work

This chapter consists of four spider diagrams or mind-maps, to enable you to consider how you can link gardening activities to the curriculum through the year.

At the centre of the diagrams are the themes of: 'Pumpkins', 'Seeds, 'Birds' and 'Market garden'. They are also available on the CD-ROM.

The ideas are suggestions, but you may be able to find many other links. They demonstrate how the whole curriculum can be met through horticulture-related activities.

Scheme of work: Pumpkin

Food technology
Use seeds, pumpkin flesh or flowers in sweet or savoury recipes.
Use spices to cook spicy pumpkin soup and serve in a hollowed-out pumpkin.

ICT
Record changes to pumpkin size, with graphs.
Produce recipe leaflets to sell.
Do research.

Literacy
Keep a diary of the pumpkin from seed to rot.
Pumpkins featured in stories.
Develop a vocabulary relating to the sensory nature of a pumpkin and seeds and use to develop poems.
Links to Halloween if permitted.

Music
Collect and dry seeds and use to make shakers, with plastic bottles or small tins.
Make music to accompany stories and poems, using the pumpkin as a drum.

Science
Life cycle: how to grow and make bigger, for competition?
Decomposition of the flesh, watch over time.
Seed collection: sowing, floating and sinking of seeds and pumpkin.

Humanities
Investigate where, geographically, pumpkins originate from, and what conditions they grow in.
Discover when pumpkins were first introduced to UK.

Maths
Estimate then measure the growth, weight and area of the leaves. Measure the girth of the growing pumpkin.
Record changes using graphs.
Estimate and count the number of seeds.
Use pumpkin for work on weight, shape and size.

RE/PSHE
Show how pumpkins feature in the culture and festivals of different countries.

Art and DT
Use mixed media to record observations of the plant, the fruit, flower and leaves. Make rubbings from the leaves or pumpkin itself. Use pâpier-maché or clay to make a 3D pumpkin model. What could be put inside a hollow papier-mâché pumpkin? Take photographs and use for a display (including a science and maths investigation into how the plant changes and grows). Problem-solving activity: how to lift or transport a heavy pumpkin?

© Becky Pinniger 2015 | *How to garden and grow: gardening as therapy for children with SEND* | LDA | Permission to photocopy

Scheme of work: Seeds

Humanities
How and why communities develop and can be sustained.
How people, communities and places are connected.
Explorers and discoverers.
Food around the world.

ICT
Present information and data.
Produce 'how to grow' leaflets.
Design a seed packet.
Do research.

Literacy
Keep a diary of the growth of a seed, such as a sunflower.
Write for a range of purposes, e.g. writing labels and instructions.
Recording, sequencing a process.
Decode a seed packet, write information for a seed packet.
Stories involving seeds and growth.

Art and music
Observational drawing using different media.
Printing, pattern-making using seeds to inspire or to print with.
Collage: 3D representation using clay or papier-mâché.
Use seeds to make percussion instruments.

Maths
Counting, measuring length of rows, weighing.
Interpret data.
Calculate percentage of germination.
Cost of seeds and producing plants.
Area, perimeter of growing space.

Food technology
Diet and nutrition related to seeds.
Recipes using seeds (e.g. spices, grains, cereals).
Bread making.

DT
Gadgets to aid seed sowing: testing manufactured ones and devising their own.

Science
The life-cycle of plants.
Seeds and conditions for growth.
Different kinds of soil.
Seed dispersal in nature.
The seasons.
Seeds as food and for other uses (e.g. jewellery, containers, instruments).

RE/PSHE
Parables involving seeds, stories in religious texts and teachings relating to seeds and personal growth.
Sex education.
Nurturing of a new plant grown from seed, related to nurturing ourselves and others.
Work as a team.

© Becky Pinniger 2015 I How to garden and grow: gardening as therapy for children with SEND I LDA I Permission to photocopy

Scheme of work: Birds

Music and movement
Use recorded birdsong to inspire and provide backdrop for children's own composition and music-making.
Use wind instruments or instruments of their own making to create 'birdsong'.
Listen to music inspired by birds, e.g. 'Lark Ascending' by Vaughan Williams. Use to encourage dance and movement.

RE/PSHE
Life-cycle of birds, how young birds are nurtured, relate to humans.
How people use birds in farming and sport.
Birds as deities, symbols.

Art and DT
Create 2D birds using card and feathers.
Make collage to hang from twigs.
Draw birds from observation, pictures using mixed media.
Make 3D birds using clay and papier-mâché.
Use basic bird shape to create cut-paper patterns on paper.
Collage of birds cut from Christmas cards and magazines.
Make prints using feathers, create headdresses.
Design bird houses, building 'nests' and feeders.

Literacy
Write descriptions of different birds, words to describe their plumage, shape and song.
Write poems and stories about birds.
Writing for a purpose: to encourage people to care for and feed birds during winter.
Write 'news reports' of bird sightings.

Humanities
Migration of birds, use map to plot route.
Birds from different countries, relate to climate.
Darwin's theories (*Origin of Species*) and bird studies.

Maths
Record numbers of birds, counting during different times of day and seasons.
Record weather and relate to bird sightings.
Maths involved in construction of bird tables, bird houses.
Weighing and measuring out bird food to fill containers.

ICT
Present and interpret data.
Produce posters to help with identification of garden birds, or to promote care for birds.
Do research.

Science
Bird skeleton and structure.
Feathers and flight.
Different beaks for different diets. Relate bird food to plants in the garden.
Feeding birds. Making bird food. Choose plants to grow for them to feed on.
What birds use to make their nests, how they build them.

Scheme of work: Market garden

Maths
Count seeds, plants and rows.
Measure the area, length of rows.
Weigh produce.
Money skills, prices.
Percentage profit, data handling.

Music
Market-sellers' cries – link with history.
Write their own to suit the produce they are selling.

Literacy
Talking and listening: plan project together.
Market research, identifying most popular fruit or vegetables in group.
Develop descriptive vocabulary, size, shape, colour, comparison, taste.
Write plans for what is to be grown. Write out recipes.
Record progress.
Persuasive writing, selling produce.
Write the diary of a market gardener.
Stories and songs related to plants and growing.

Humanities
The historical and geographical origin of plants and foods.
Markets around the world: how they compare, what produce they sell.

Art and DT
Observational drawings of fruit and vegetables, which can be used on posters.
Decorate pots in which to grow produce.
Create boxes or other containers in which to sell produce.
Make flower arrangements and posies to sell.
Use fruit and vegetables to make dyes.
Print using vegetables, e.g. posters or printed aprons.

IT
Use to make posters advertising produce.
Create price labels.
Produce graphs to show amount of produce grown, profit, etc.
Search for recipes to use with produce.
Do research.

Market garden

Food technology
Nutrition and diet.
Cooking with fruit and vegetables, and their nutritional value.

Science
Parts of plants and their function.
Growing requirements of plants.
Cycle of life.
Nitrogen cycle, making compost and use for compost.

GLOSSARY

General terms

Attention restoration This is the process which Kaplan and Kaplan (1989) proposed can occur in nature. They observed that because nature is fundamentally interesting and stimulating but requires no effort to be in, it can have a restorative function for those whose mind is 'fatigued'. They noted that minds become fatigued when trying to focus on a specific task or instruction if this is accompanied by other distractions. Kaplan and Kaplan maintain that nature is consequently *restorative* for a mind that is fatigued by too much directed attention.

Backward chaining This is a technique used to enable those who cannot fulfil a complete process, to engage in the *end* of the task, and gradually learn the whole process by working *backwards* through the steps. This gives them a sense of achievement and an initial success.

Fine motor skills These use smaller muscle groups to perform more specific tasks than gross motor skills (see below), such as sowing seeds, opening packets, tying plants and writing labels.

Gross motor skills These involve large muscle groups and include tasks such as walking, lifting, pushing and raking. See also 'Fine motor skills'.

Horticultural therapy This is the application of horticulture to meet a person's particular need.

Hypersensitivity When a child has a high level of sensitivity.

Hyposensitivity When a child has a low level of sensitivity.

Makaton This is a language programme using signs and symbols to enable people to communicate. It is designed to support spoken language, and the signs and symbols can be used with speech.

PECS (Picture Exchange Communication System) It was devised for those with autism or related developmental disabilities, to encourage and enable communication.

Proprioceptive system This is the system responsible for sensing the movement of one's body and making a person aware of the position of their limbs and joints, in space, without needing to look. Proprioception is sometimes referred to as the 'sixth sense'.

Sensory stories These are aimed specifically at the needs of children with PMLD. Simple stories are told using props designed to stimulate all five senses to fit with the story. They may be used repeatedly to enable the child to anticipate the stimulus they are about to receive.

SCRUFFY targets These targets are: Student-led; Creative; Relevant; Unspecified; Fun; For Youngsters (Lacey, 2010).

SMART targets These targets are: Specific; Measurable; Achievable; Relevant; Time-bound.

Task analysis This is a process used by staff to determine the individual steps involved in carrying out a specific task, such as planting a bulb. It can be used to determine the ability of a child to carry out the task, and also to assess their ability in doing so.

Therapeutic horticulture This is the therapeutic effect, be it passive or active, that gardens and gardening can have on a person's wellbeing.

Vestibular system The vestibular system is the sensory system chiefly responsible for providing a sense of balance and spatial awareness, which are needed for balance and co-ordination.

Widget symbols These symbols replace words in written text to enable non-readers to communicate.

Gardening terms

Annual An annual is a plant that sets seed, flowers and dies within one year, such as basil, tomatoes, Californian poppy (*Eschscholzia*) and love-in-a-mist (*Nigella*).

Biennial A plant which grows over two years – sown one year and usually flowering or fruiting the next, e.g. parsley, foxglove (*Digitalis*) and wallflower (*Erysimum*)

Biodegradable This describes something that can be decomposed through biological means. It rots down through the action of bacteria and fungi.

Cell trays (also known as '**modules**') These are plastic trays with individual cells to hold plants. Many plants are sold in these and they can be re-used. They come in a variety of sizes to hold plants at different stages of growth.

Chitting To chit potatoes is to put them in a light, cool place for the buds to begin to grow, prior to planting. Once small shoots have formed from the buds, the potatoes are considered ready for planting out. There is debate among gardeners about the benefits of this process. Potatoes can grow without being chitted first, but the yield may not be as great.

Chlorophyll This is the scientific name for the green-coloured chemical in plants that is involved in photosynthesis.

Cold frame These are usually low structures made from a wooden or metal frame with glass or perspex, into which plants are placed which need protection from the weather, before they are planted into the ground.

Compost Purchased compost is used as a soil substitute and comes in different forms. Some may be sold as seed-sowing compost; other forms are multi-purpose, or specifically for trees and shrubs. The consistency and constituents will be different. Alternatively, compost can refer to the dark material produced when well-rotted organic matter is heaped together as part of the gardening process, for example vegetable scraps, grass cuttings, chopped-up prunings, card and paper.

Coppicing This is the process of cutting down branches of a tree or shrub to ground level. This encourages new branches to form, which in turn can be coppiced in three to four years' time. The resulting branches are useful for building fences or structures to use in the garden, for example with hazel or willow.

'Cut and come again' is the term given to describe salad varieties which can be harvested repeatedly. The outer leaves are harvested, allowing the small inner leaves to grow, which are in turn harvested. The plant can be harvested for several weeks before becoming exhausted.

Cuttings Taking cuttings is the process of removing a small part of a parent plant and placing it in soil to form a new plant (see Chapter 2).

Dead-heading This describes the process of removing dead flowers from a plant. This encourages the plant to continue flowering, instead of setting seeds.

Deciduous Plants which lose their leaves in the autumn are known as 'deciduous'. Oak and ash are examples of deciduous trees.

Dividing Perennials which have formed large clumps may be dug up and split into two or more parts, each bearing some root. This is called 'dividing'. The subsequent pieces can all be replanted and will grow on to make more plants.

Evergreen Plants that do not lose their leaves in winter are evergreens, for example fir trees and holly.

Fleece This is a fine, translucent fabric usually in white, which is used to protect tender plants from frost. Ground can be covered in fleece to retain warmth in the soil and enable soil to warm up in the spring.

Forcing By giving plants protection from the elements, and extra care, they can be brought into fruit or flower early – or 'forced'. This is sometimes done with plants such as rhubarb; rhubarb may be covered up to encourage young stems to be ready to pick before the main crop.

Hardening off This is the process by which plants and seedlings that have been raised indoors are gradually acclimatised to harder conditions outside.

Hardy Plants are described as 'hardy' when they are able to withstand winter temperatures without needing any sort of protection, for example holly, apple trees, buddleja, leeks, garlic and broad beans.

Leaf mould This is produced when leaves, collected in the autumn, have broken down (usually over two years). If really well rotted and crumbly, this mould can be sieved and used as seed-sowing compost. If less well rotted, it can be added to the soil to improve its condition.

Lifting This means to dig plants up out of the ground. Lifting potatoes is what you do when it is time to harvest them; lifting perennials is what you do when you want to divide them.

Micro-greens This is a relatively new term, used to describe the initial leaves produced by seeds on germination, which can be harvested and used in salads. They have a high nutritional value and intensity of taste. Seeds such as herbs, beetroot, cabbage, pea shoots and spinach can be grown and harvested this way. They take one or two weeks to grow, so can be good for children who like to see quick results. Seeds collected from your own crops can be used for this. ☠ Do not use parsnip seeds though, because they are poisonous.

Modules (also known as '**cell trays**') This is the name given to plastic trays with individual cells to hold plants. Many plants are sold in these and they can be re-used. They come in a variety of sizes to hold plants at different stages of growth.

Mulch This is used to cover soil to prevent weeds from growing and to retain moisture. It may be in the form of bark chippings, slate chips, gravel, pebbles or plastic sheeting. It can also be used to enhance the appearance of a bed or container.

Node   The node of a plant is the part of the stem where a leaf joins it.

Nutrients   These are the minerals absorbed from the soil by the plant. They are phosphorus, nitrogen and potassium. Some may be applied to plants if their growth, flowering or fruiting needs to be improved, using purchased 'food' or by making food from nettles or comfrey (see 'Feeding plants' in Chapter 2). Applying too much to encourage growth can lead to problems, such as lack of fruit or flowers.

Organic gardening   Synthetic chemicals are not used in organic gardening. Instead, the gardener works with nature, for example encouraging ladybirds, which are the natural predators of greenfly, rather than spraying chemicals against these pests. Food from plants and broken-down organic matter (home-made compost) are used to promote healthy plants.

Perennial   This is a plant which is able to live over several years, often dying down in winter but remaining alive underground, ready to appear in spring.

Perlite   A small white mineral added to compost to improve aeration and water retention, often used when making cuttings or sowing seeds.

Plug plants   These small plants are produced and made available commercially. They are larger than a newly grown seedling. They have been grown in special modules, ready for planting out, or potting on if they are in a small module.

Positive psychology   This approach concentrates on improving a child's emotional and social wellbeing and making a child happy.

Potting on   This is the process of putting a plant which has outgrown its space in a small pot into a larger pot so that it can increase in size.

Pricking out   This is when seedlings are removed from their small growing space in a seed tray or pot, and instead are put into a larger container to grow on (see Chapter 2).

Propagation   This is the process by which new plants are produced from pieces of an original plant, by taking cuttings or by sowing its seeds.

Pruning   This is the process of removing parts of a plant to enhance growth, or to enhance flower and fruit production. It can also be used to reduce the size of a plant that has outgrown its space.

Raised beds   These are growing spaces contained by wooden or other supports, and filled with good soil or compost. They can enable those with a physical disability to garden more easily, and enable improved soil to be used in areas where soil is poor.

Succulents   These are plants whose fleshy leaves contain water, and enable them to survive drought conditions, for example cacti and sedums.

Staking   Plants which may not be able to grow securely without support may need staking. A stake is usually a firm piece of wood, bought specifically for the purpose. Young trees often need staking when they are first put in. Some perennials which grow very tall, such as delphiniums, may need staking.

Stratifying   This is the process in which tree seeds are kept in cold, damp soil and given frosty conditions to break their dormancy and encourage them to break into growth in the spring.

Tender   Plants are described as tender when they are unable to withstand temperatures below freezing, e.g. tomatoes, French marigolds and sunflowers. They are grown outside during the spring and summer after the danger of frost has passed, and in the protection of a heated greenhouse during the colder months.

Weed-suppressant membrane   This membrane is sold in garden centres by the metre. It is made in different thicknesses and is used to cover areas of ground to suppress the growth of weeds. It is useful to cover paths between raised beds, and can then be covered in bark mulch. If you have an area of ground you are not ready to cultivate, then it is useful for keeping weeds down until you are ready to use that area. It can also be used to line raised beds to deter weeds.

Wormery   A wormery is a relatively small bin or container, which contains special red worms to enable food waste to be converted quickly into compost. If space is limited, this may be a more viable option than a compost heap.

SOURCES OF INFORMATION

I do recommend visiting gardens and garden shows. In recent years there have been garden designs aimed at children and, more recently, at specific disabilities, including children with SEND. These can be a great source of ideas and inspiration.

Websites*

There are thousands of helpful sites on the internet. Probably the best one to start with is the Royal Horticultural Society (RHS) (www.rhs.org.uk/). Its website is a mine of useful information and guidance, plus offers for schools.

https://schoolgardening.rhs.org.uk/home

Join the excellent Campaign for School Gardening to receive many useful resources, take part in competitions, and find out about its training courses for CPD.

The following websites are arranged in alphabetical order.

www.activehands.com

This company sells gripping aids for a variety of purposes, and for all ages.

www.artnet.com/artists/andy-goldsworthy

Here you can discover and be inspired by the art of well-known artist Andy Goldsworthy, who creates ephemeral art outside, using natural objects.

www.asdan.org.uk

Promotes active learning and enables young people to develop skills for learning and employment. Enables those with different learning styles to take part in courses designed to develop their personal and employability skills through a range of subjects, including horticulture.

www.barfusspark.info/en

For information and ideas on creating a barefoot path.

www.brilliantgardenproducts.co.uk

This organisation supplies RADIUS tools, which are lighter and ergonomically designed to reduce muscle fatigue and stress.

www.carryongardening.org.uk

This site is connected with Thrive (a registered charity using social and therapeutic horticulture to benefit those with a disability), and is a useful source of advice and ideas for making gardening easier for people of all ages touched by disability.

All website addresses were correct at the time of going to print.

www.classideas.co.uk
A source of personalised motivational wristbands.

www.edenproject.com
Provides ideas for play, lesson plans and learning resources.

www.farmgarden.org.uk
The Federation of City Farms and Community Gardens supports the use of farming and gardening as an educational tool and promotes the benefits of learning outside the normal classroom environment.

www.flowerpotman.com/disabledgardening
Some good suggestions for adapting tools to suit different needs for adults, which could be applicable when working with children.

www.foodforlife.org.uk
This organisation encourages healthy eating in schools and has many excellent resources for teachers. Look for growing cards in teachers' resources. These are very clear and could be useful for the new gardener, with all necessary advice on the plant clearly set out. More able learners could find them useful too. If printed out, they could be a good resource to help children choose the plants they want to grow in their own plot.

www.foresteducation.org
Information on using trees and woodlands with children. This is the site for Outdoor Woodland Learning (OWL) Scotland.

www.fruitfulschools.com
Information and 'orchard packs' to enable schools to grow their own orchard.

www.gardenorganic.org.uk
This site is full of ideas and resources to enable you to garden organically. Garden Organic also runs courses at Ryton Gardens near Coventry, Warwickshire.

www.gardeningwithchildren.co.uk
Designed as 'an interactive classroom, allotment plot and hobby garden', and has some resources for school gardening. It is linked with Recycle Works (www.therecycleworks.co.uk).

www.greengardener.co.uk
A range of gardening products, including organic pest control and plant foods.

www.growcareers.info
Information on careers in horticulture. Set up by leading organisations within the horticulture industry.

www.growingschools.org.uk
This site has many useful resources and ideas to help get children growing.

www.herbsociety.org.uk/schools/index.htm
Specific information for KS1 and KS2, and some pages for teachers. Includes links to the curriculum. All activities are based around herbs.

www.ltl.org.uk
Learning Through Landscapes encourages the development of stimulating outdoor spaces for children. By registering with them, you have access to some good resources and CPD opportunities. Lots of information about the benefits of being outdoors.

www.naturedetectives.org.uk

A range of excellent, free, downloadable resources, which can provide teachers with plenty of ideas.

www.nocn.org.uk

Information about accredited horticulture qualifications with a step-by-step, unit-by-unit route from Entry Level up to Level 4. The qualifications can lead to an award or certificate-level qualification, enabling learners to increase their confidence and employability.

www.nurturegroups.org

Support, information and training on nurture groups for children and young people who present particularly challenging behaviour in school.

www.peta-uk.com

Adapted and special gardening tools for those with disabilities (also see the Thrive website for more information on equipment and tools to help those with disabilities).

www.playassociation.org.uk/new-charter-for-children's-play

You can find here *The New Charter for Children's Play* (1998).

www.potatoesforschools.org.uk

Participate in the 'Grow Your Own Potatoes' projects to receive free seed potatoes and lots of ideas and worksheets aimed at both mainstream children and children with SEND.

www.rhs.org.uk/movingupgrowingon

Find out about a special project that the RHS carried out, working with young people with special needs, and discover the positive results that ensued.

www.rocketgardens.co.uk

Has a section for school gardens. They sell packs of ready-to-plant vegetable plugs – an expensive but effective way to make a start.

www.rspb.org.uk/wildlife/wildlifegarden/

Information and resources relating to birds and other garden wildlife, aimed at children.

www.sensorytrust.org.uk

The Sensory Trust website has information and ideas on creating a 'sensory garden' and is a very useful site for those wanting more information on developing children's sensory experience outside. Try '**gofindit**' a new simple card game that the Trust has developed, which is 'a fun way to discover any outdoor environment using all the senses'.

www.tcv.org.uk/

Provides information on the TCV 'Green Gym' initiative. The TVC helps people to reclaim green places through different environmental projects.

www.thegrowingschoolsgarden.co.uk

This is an interactive website inspired by the Growing Schools Garden at Birmingham Botanic Gardens. It has resources, photos, videos, instructions and useful links.

www.therecycleworks.co.uk

Sells raised beds, compost bins, and so on. There is a section on children's gardens and for those with disabilities.

www.teachernet.gov.uk/growingschools

Designed to support teachers in using the 'outdoor classroom' as a teaching resource for all ages. It has resources for SEND too. Look up nature play recipes for some novel, and at times wonderfully messy, ideas for outside play and exploration. Useful information for those working with children with emotional difficulties too.

www.thrive.org.uk – see www.carryongardening.org.uk.

www.wiggleywigglers.co.uk

Information on composting, wormeries, caring for wildlife and wildlife gardening.

www.woodlandtrust.org.uk

Schools can apply for packs of free trees. There are also many useful resources relating to trees and wildlife available to download. Useful for games and other activities.

www.verticalveg.org.uk/how-to-make-your-own-wormery

This is an excellent site explaining how to make and use a wormery, with tips on where to find the worms.

Books

This short list deals mostly with books related to specific needs of children or adults with SEND; it does not contain the titles of general books for gardening for adults or children, as there is such a vast selection.

A Sensory Curriculum for Very Special People (F Longhorn; Souvenir Press, 1995): a practical approach to curriculum planning for children with PMLD.

Gardening for Children with Autistic Spectrum Disorders and Special Needs (N Etherington; Jessica Kingsley, 2012): a very good introduction to using horticulture as therapy for children.

Green Spaces. Outdoor environments for adults with autism (K Gaurion and C McGinley; Kingwood Trust, 2012; available at www.kingwood.org.uk): an excellent booklet with many relevant ideas to suit children, and those with different educational needs to autism.

Grow It, Eat It (Dorling Kindersley, 2008): a growing and cooking book aimed at children, but with clear pictures and good suggestions. Good for the novice gardener, young or old. (Similar books are also produced by the RHS; see the RHS Campaign for School Gardening (www.rhs.org.uk/schoolgardening) for other available titles.)

Nature's Playground (F Danks and J Schofield; Frances Lincoln Ltd, 2005): there are several other books available on the same theme by these authors.

Poisonous Plants – A guide for parents and childcare providers (E A Dauncey; Kew Publishing, 2010): an excellent guide for non-gardeners, with clear pictures to help with identification and text suitable for non-professional gardeners.

The Playground Potting Shed (D Murphy; Guardian Books, 2008): although not aimed at children with SEND, there is good horticultural advice and suggestions for plants which fit in with the school year. The author has experience of running school gardening clubs.

REFERENCES

Department for Education (DfE) (2015) *Special Educational Needs and Disability Code of Practice: 0 to 25 years*. DfE.

Department for Education and Skills (DfES) (2006) *Learning Outside the Classroom Manifesto*. DfES Publications.

Hussein H (2010) Using the sensory garden as a tool to enhance the educational development and social interaction of children with special needs. *Support for Learning*, 25 (1), 25–31. Nasen.

Kaplan R and Kaplan S (1989) *The Experience of Nature. A psychological perspective*. Cambridge University Press.

Lacey P (2010) SMART and SCRUFFY targets. *SLD Experience*, 57, Summer 2010, 16–21.

Mental Health Foundation (1999) *Brighter Futures: Promoting children and young people's mental health*. Mental Health Foundation.

Moore RC and Wong HH (1997) *Natural Learning: The life history of an environmental schoolyard: creating environments for rediscovering nature's way of teaching*. MIG Communications.

National Children's Bureau (1992) *A Charter for Children's Play*. National Voluntary Council for Children's Play.

Wilson EO (1984) *Biophilia*. Cambridge: Harvard University Press.

NOTES